T0265510

# THE DATA DELUGE

ARUN C. KUMAR

# THE DATA DELUGE

## MAKING MARKETING WORK FOR BRANDS AND PEOPLE

Forbes | Books

Published by Forbes Books, Charleston, South Carolina.
An imprint of Advantage Media Group.



Printed in the United States of America.

10 9 8 7 6 5 4 3 2 1

ISBN: 979-8-88750-335-6 (Hardcover)
ISBN: 979-8-88750-336-3 (eBook)

Library of Congress Control Number: 2023924426

Cover design by Megan Elger.
Layout design by Ruthie Wood.

*To Aadu, Snoopy, and Achala for being my soul mates in this amazing journey.*

## CONTENTS

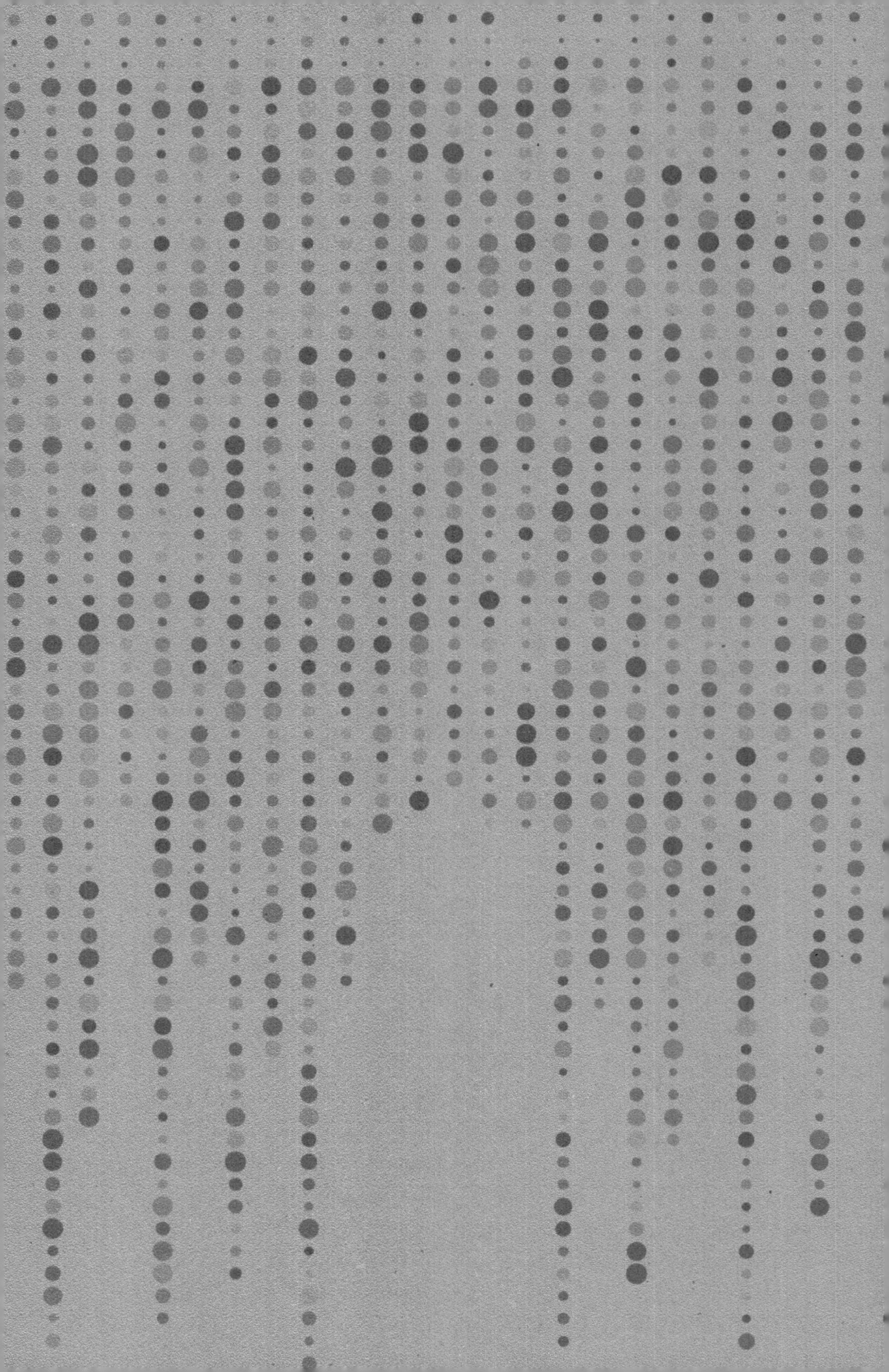

# ACKNOWLEDGMENTS

Usually I thought, this is the easiest bit to write, but how wrong I was! It is hard to accurately represent the incredible generosity and time that I was given by some of the busiest people in the industry.

I'd like to thank all the people who spoke to me for this book; their interviews are spread across various chapters, and I would not have had this depth of understanding of many issues without their help. Special thanks to Bob Liodice, CEO of the ANA, Kevin Krim, CEO of EDO Inc., Greg Stuart of the MMA, and Andrea Brimmer, CMO of Ally Financial for opening their doors to great thinking. I'm indebted to John Chirapurath of SAP for talking to me about the value of data in product design. His was the one perspective that gave a peek behind the scenes of a tech company willing to leverage data for a better user experience.

Another person who helped me understand TV and its further evolution in the connected TV space is Krishan Bhatia, former president of NBC Universal. Krishan and I have had many conversations, and he is one of the few people in the industry where I feel like I can start a conversation and it would be like carrying on from where we left off.

My ex-team members have contributed immensely, and you can find them in these pages. A big thank you to Ian Johnson, Saqib Mausoof, and Michael Heberle.

This section would be poorer for not giving thanks to the efforts of Matt Seiler, head of executive services at Banff, to connect me to many people and get a better-informed perspective. Last but not least is my love and affection for my deceased mentor V. Ramani, who instilled a love and curiosity of data in me.

# CHAPTER ONE

# The Silent Colosseum and the Noisy Bar

I received yet another email from the online travel booking site. Apparently, they wanted to help me complete my flight booking to Paris. In an ideal world, I would have embraced this and loved the fact that my data trail had led to an anticipation of my needs with a possible conclusion that was deeply satisfying and ended with me eating macaroons in a Parisian cafe. However, all I felt was frustration and anger. I had just spent a tidy packet booking business-class seats to Paris for me and my family on the same site just minutes before. Yes, I had tried multiple combinations over many days, but I *had* converted! I bought the damn tickets, didn't I? Surely, that meant somewhere in some system, I should have been recognized as a conversion, a customer, or a person who didn't need any more reminders of his desire to book tickets to Paris.

I entered the advertising industry twenty-five years ago, spent most of my time in media, the last ten in programmatic or addressable media buying, and the last seven, additionally, on the resulting data explosion and how to integrate it into marketing, all with the hope of solving problems like the above. During this time, I also witnessed tremendous change in the craft of marketing over multiple markets and geographies.

In 1998, India was in the throes of a recession when I entered the industry as a media planner. It forced me to confront cost management in a risk-averse environment, where squeezing efficiencies and getting more bang for your buck was the only variable of success. In addition, India—with regional dialects and cultural differences across the country—was a very complicated case, including a variety of media. As I moved on in my career, China in 2005 was a complete contrast; it was a booming economy with few systems in place but also a complicated market that was still trying to formulate methodologies to accurately calculate media reach and frequency and one that relied on expats to set the standard.

Next, in 2008, Singapore was where I learned how to operate across cultures and budgets in a regional role where some markets resisted the idea of centralization, and others wanted the regional center to completely run the show. In 2013, the United Kingdom was a shock to the system; I was now dealing with marketing budgets for certain brands that would have been the total Asia-Pacific ad spend for all brands in a quarter across the agency. I was responsible for markets in Western Europe, Latin America, and Asia-Pacific. The cultural and spend differences were dizzying.

Ultimately, I landed in the United States in 2015, and my transformation was complete. I had gone from recession to opportunity, managing a mixed bag, and finally the world with the United States at the center.

Along the way, I started looking at my industry in a big-picture sense, and I realized we had significant problems—as anyone who has received digital ads over . . . and over . . . and over again can testify to. Not just repetitive ads but ones that are oftentimes not even useful to us or that miss the mark. I also love disruption and change. I have never been comfortable with the status quo. And I love marketing and advertising because as an industry it tends to reward disruption since ideation is a fundamental currency. I have experienced both humbling lows and ecstatic highs while taking massive leaps—and I wouldn't have it any other way. I love to call myself a pirate and have often branded my teams the same way. I collected an amazing bunch of people over the years who wanted to break things, make them better, and do them in iconoclastic ways.

And unlike a true pirate captain, I likened myself to the lookout posted on the mast. Come rain or shine, I was there chasing treasure and directing crews to change course over impending storms. I was right up there when the storms came barreling toward us, and I enjoyed the spoils of loot up in my lonely post on the mast.

And yet, I witnessed the promised land and/or loot-laden ships sliding past my portside like specks on the horizon despite my furious attempts at navigation, shouting down from my crow's nest, waving my hands and pointing at the rocks and the channels we needed to pass through to get to our treasures safely.

I was no stranger to the promises we as a collective industry had made to people and society at large. As digital platforms scaled, data exhaust scaled, and the possibilities were exciting and endless.

These magnificent promises went something like this: Share your personal information and we will make your experiences and interactions meaningful so much so that you will love this new world. It will be automated, trustworthy, and very precise. We will know about you and respect you and care about your preferences. You won't have to see meaningless ads for products you don't want or care about, and this will be coupled with knowledge that will empower us to serve up interesting entertainment, brands, and cultural experiences tailored to you.

We promised or believed that data and the digital revolution that produced it would take marketing to new heights. Chief marketing officers (CMOs) and CEOs were convinced by technology platforms, data providers, data brokers, and analytics companies that this new world would be worth investing in. And the investment came in from multiple places. Almost a trillion dollars' worth of spend behind marketing with almost 60 percent of that going into digital channels. If you removed the United States and other advanced markets, the digital percentages would drop.

In 2018, when I played a key role in the acquisition of Acxiom for IPG (Interpublic Group), and when we began the process of integrating it into our digital marketing and advertising capabilities across all agencies in the group, I believed that we had made a step change in our approach to making marketing more meaningful. I still believe that it was transformative.

And yet, if I put on my hat as a consumer, as a person who was just on the receiving end of digital marketing, I would be angry, annoyed, and frustrated with many advertising and marketing efforts. In March 2021, in a survey of US internet users and their thoughts about ads online, 22.6 percent reported that they hated ads. A mere 1.1 percent reported that they liked ads.[1]

I decided to come down from my lofty perch atop the mast and go down into the very depths of the ship and figure out why the efforts to make marketing better and advertising more meaningful had failed. And I realized that while I had been busy focusing on the promised

---

1 Audrey Schomer, "Consumer attitudes toward digital advertising 2021 - insider intelligence trends, forecasts & statistics," eMarketer, July 22, 2021, accessed October 12, 2023, https://www.insiderintelligence.com/content/consumer-attitudes-toward-digital-advertising-2021.

land and the myriad ships where our treasure was borne, I had lost touch with those small shifts in current, the waves that prodded us away from our direction, and the differing interests of the crew, which meant that we were working at cross-purposes.

This book is one of discovery—both for leaders of business and for me. I've tried to take both the view from the crow's nest and the view from the deck, as well as the view from the engine room, of the various factors impacting marketing and integrate them into one construct. And in order to rededicate myself to the promised land of relevance and consent, respect and entertainment, where people tolerated ads because they found them relevant and sometimes even enjoyed them because the ads spoke to them, made them laugh, or were for a product they genuinely needed or wanted.

Before we begin this journey though, let's get some definitions straight because marketing and advertising are two terms that keep getting used interchangeably even though they are not the same.

Philip Kotler, in 2018, defined marketing as the "process by which companies engage customers, build strong customer relationships, and create customer value in order to capture value from customers in return."[2] Advertising is a marketing tactic; it's an act of promotion that involves paying for space where messages can seek to influence people. Advertising budgets are part of marketing budgets. Marketing budgets also include PR, events, promotions, marketing technology investments, creative production, celebrity endorsements,

---

2 Martin Himli, "Street Food Vendors' Entrepreneurial Marketing Characteristics and Practices from 12 Countries: What Lessons Can Be Learnt for Improving Food Marketing in BOP/Subsistence Marketplaces," Middle East Journal of Agriculture Research 9, no. 2 (June 2020): 321-348, DOI:10.36632/mejar/2020.9.2.27, https://www.researchgate.net/publication/341942086_Street_food_vendors%27_entrepreneurial_marketing_characteristics_and_practices_from_12_countries_what_lessons_can_be_learnt_for_improving_food_marketing_in_BOPSubsistence_marketplaces#pf7.

sports sponsorships, direct marketing, and the like. Because marketers advertise and because paid advertising is a large expense in most marketing budgets, the two words are often used interchangeably.

The other reality is that these budgets don't necessarily sit in the same place. There might be a marketing budget under the CMO, and multiple budgets underpinning those efforts that sit under the chief information officer (CIO), who makes marketing technology decisions in certain organizations, or the chief digital officer or chief data officer (CDO), who may have separate budgets to help support marketing efforts.

But I focus on the sum total of all marketing efforts because consumers do not differentiate or classify channels. They get an impression (or not) about a product or a brand based on all efforts, not just that of paid advertising. There are very limited, accurate estimates of marketing budgets; mostly it's ad budgets that get tracked and focused on.

This is also why I frequently use terms such as marketing and advertising interchangeably. As a CMO, one might make distinctions between the PR budget and a media budget for advertising; the consumer doesn't and therefore I don't either.

Back to my journey of discovery.

As I indicated, advertising, which was supposed to have become markedly better over the last few years, has worsened. Take any measure, and you will see ad avoidance at a high. In a June 2021 survey conducted by Hub Research and cited by eMarketer, 57 percent of US TV viewers said they can tolerate some ads, but they'd abandon a service if there are too many. In addition, 17 percent said they would never sign up for an ad-supported video service.[3]

---

3 Schomer, "Consumer Attitudes Toward Digital Advertising 2021."

Adblockers are frequently used. When asked, "Which of the following online activities have you done in the last thirty days?" 38 percent of respondents said they had used an adblocker in an Integral Ad Science report done jointly with YouGov in August 2022 in the United States.[4]

On the flip side, privacy activists, regulators, and politicians have begun targeting advertising and marketing as bad actors in society, with some overcompensating for perceived excesses. This school believes in shutting down observational advertising, data collection, and eliminating many of the platforms that exist. Between Cambridge Analytica, Mark Zuckerberg's testimony to Congress, Apple's privacy claims, and the antitrust move on Google, marketing in some shape or another has provided convenient fodder for the press. Many press outlets, such as *The New York Times*, that have criticized data collection get a sizable contribution from digital advertising (61 percent of ad revenue amounting to $318 million in 2022).[5]

The irony is shocking if not ludicrous. One of my favorite pieces of research is *The Economic Impact of Advertising in the US Economy 2018-2026* conducted by IHS Markit in November 2021 for the Advertising Coalition.[6] The report identifies the combined impact of advertising expenditures, advertising-driven sales, supplier sales, interindustry sales, and sales due to employees of these firms respending some of their wages in their communities.

To quote the report,

---

4 Integral Ads, "Future of Privacy First Advertising Report," https://go.integralads.com/Privacy-First-Advertising-Research.html.

5 Amy Watson, "New York Times Company: Advertising Revenue from 2006 to 2022," Statistica, accessed May 20, 2023, https://www.statista.com/statistics/192907/advertising-revenue-of-the-new-york-times-company-since-2006/.

6 HIS Markit, "The economic impact of advertising in the US economy 2018-2026," February 4, 2022, accessed October 2, 2023.

In 2020, the US economy posted $36.7 trillion in sales activity. Of that, $2.8 trillion in sales were directly stimulated as a result of the $325.6 billion that companies spent to advertise their products and services. Thus, about 7.6 percent of US sales activity is *directly* stimulated by advertising. However, fulfilling the direct sales initiates follow-on activity throughout the economy as dollars flow through supply chains, driving an additional $2.0 trillion in *indirect* sales. The economic stimulation does not end there: companies and their suppliers hire and pay employees, who, in turn, spend some of their income in the economy on consumer goods and services. These *induced* consumer effects amounted to an additional $2.0 trillion in 2020. Thus, the initial $325.6 billion in ad spending drove an additional $6.8 trillion in sales. This equates to each dollar of ad spending in 2020 leveraging almost $21 in sales activity. The combined $7.1 trillion (ad spend + stimulated sales activity) means that 19.4 percent of the $36.7 trillion in total sales generated in the US economy was attributable to advertising expenditures in 2020.[7]

In addition, advertising supported about 19.5 percent of jobs in the United States. And they aren't bad at pay. The average salary of jobs supported by advertising was 12 percent above the national average at $73,000 a year.[8]

Many of the sentiments and proposals in the legislative space are guaranteed to eliminate some of these jobs. And that's before friendly AI (artificial intelligence) has raised its head. Most politicians struggle to understand that constraining technology platforms and observational advertising will have an impact on the economy for which we are not yet prepared.

---

7 Ibid.

8 Ibid.

And the entire marketing ecosystem is helping these legislators and politicians by either staying silent or by burying its collective head in the sand to avoid becoming the center of attention or allowing others to speak on its behalf, some of whose interests are not necessarily aligned with those of marketing. For an industry that earns its bread by helping brands communicate with people, it doesn't do a great job in telling its own story.

It's time to defend marketing and the vital role it plays in a democracy, any economy, and all our collective futures. Free press only remains free because advertising pays for content to be generated and distributed. Multiple opinions and their distribution are expensive; someone needs to pay the bill. And often consumers don't quite realize that what they pay as subscription fees is not enough to sustain content production. Ask your local TikTok creator and they will tell you how dependent they are on brand promotions and ad fees. As with most issues about our society, interconnectedness means that often the laws and policies we enact to protect ourselves are the ones that end up hurting us the most. In that respect, love and laws are quite similar.

However, a defense cannot be mounted until we in the marketing and business community accept and fix some glaring issues that have allowed people to dislike us and feel disconnected from our vision of inclusion and diversity and believe that we are in it for just ourselves.

Marketing as a profession is ripe for disruption. Between CMOs being under the gun (Professor Scott Galloway recently insisted that CMOs had about eighteen months to survive[9]), new structures where CFOs have marketing departments report to them since marketing is seen as a cost to be controlled, and the incredible risks that executives

9 Tom Fogden, "You're Dead in 18 Months or Less: Scott Galloway on the Future of CMOs," accessed October 15, 2023, https://www.bandt.com.au/youre-dead-in-18-months-or-less-scott-galloway-on-the-future-of-cmos/.

have to take to bridge societal issues, the marketing ecosystem is very interesting to say the least.

As I write this, Anheuser-Busch has put Alissa Heinerscheid, VP of marketing for Bud Light, and Daniel Blake, who looks after marketing for Anheuser-Busch's mainstream brands, on leave. Dylan Mulvaney, a transgender influencer, had posted a video on a social media account to promote a Bud Light contest. And so began a series of boycotts and buycotts that resulted in sales dropping. Both executives were harassed online and had their lives examined through an unedifying lens.

Target removed Pride Month products due to threats against employees, while Walmart took a strong stance in support of being inclusive and keeping certain merchandise in store. Starbucks workers protested managers removing Pride memorabilia from certain stores. The list goes on.

I haven't even gotten into the use of data yet or the incredible power of narrow AI tools to wreak havoc on ideation, process workflow automation, eliminate intermediaries, and clean up a supply chain that has become a trough for agencies to treat as their backstop for all the commitments made to their clients.

Most importantly, the tale of the following (fill in product) remains. If you're an adult who shops online, you've probably experienced this at some stage. You chose shoes, airline tickets, lingerie, or cat food and decided not to buy it and left the cart behind. And then everyone in your household just saw ads for lingerie for the next month. You have to ask yourself: if marketing was so sophisticated, and we knew everything about consumers, how did we not know when to stop harassing people?

To begin to understand the mess we have created and find ourselves in, I invite you to step into the worlds of the Silent Colosseum and the Noisy Bar. I deliberately chose these terms with contrasts to mirror both the sizes of the two constituents and the fact that you get to hear so much more from the smaller set that claims to represent a large swath of society without truly doing so.

In the Silent Colosseum, you will find a varied set of characters ranging from marketers, agencies, technology platforms, data management companies, social platforms, media companies, and consultants of all ilk.

In the Noisy Bar, you will find privacy activists, regulators, politicians, industry associations, lobbying groups, and the media, which often finds itself challenged to understand this space and indeed sources of its own funding that enables its existence.

Between the silence of the colosseum and the noise of the bar with its narrow focus on rights seen through an even narrower lens stand the rest of us (I'll put myself in this group for the moment), the consumers and viewers of advertising, the targets of marketing—frustrated by what they experience, dismissive of many brands, appreciative of the free content they find online or "cheaper" streaming options for content, with little knowledge of the economics driving content creation and distribution.

Marketing is hugely satisfying; it's also hugely irritating and avoidable at times. But if you follow the money, there is no denying that many aspects of democracy are funded by marketing, and it is such an important barometer of our culture.

Getting the colosseum to speak or communicate with one voice and quieting the bar a bit might help both sides to understand each other a bit better. You must understand the colosseum and the bar first to fix them.

# The Silent Colosseum

## PLAYER 1: THE MARKETERS

Marketers are increasingly expected to play multiple roles. I got a firsthand taste of this when I was invited to attend the Forbes Most Influential CMOs luncheon in Cannes in June 2023 by the ever-gracious Seth Matlins, managing director of the Forbes CMO Council. In a room full of the top CMOs of the world in the Carlton hotel on the Croisette, the themes were striking. Most CMOs spoke about the changing demands placed on their time. Their roles ranged from having to guide the organization through digital transformation, retail transformation, and the rise of AI to managing risk by avoiding social gaffes and respecting privacy—all this while inspiring people to engage with their brands and buy them using thought-provoking ideas and creativity. And before you take a breath, they have to do this with multiple partners and vendors, technology providers and agencies in the mix, many of whom would rather step on each other's toes than do the tango.

What went unstated in the room that day was the expectations placed by their bosses who increasingly included CFOs. And most of those expectations centered around growth, sales, or some variant of that. Critical to meeting that expectation is the ability to tie brand building and media budgets to business outcomes.

Why is it so hard to quantify the success of marketing, brand building, and the like? That's a whole book in and of itself (welcome to this one!), but marketing faces the trouble with accurately quantifying its contribution to sales. We will examine this later, but this fundamental issue creates a chain of consequences. It's a vicious cycle: if you cannot prove your value conclusively, you become a cost, and a big line item at that. Hence, over the last decade or so, procurement has become more involved, and decisions around marketing are led by cost control.

Combined with this is the fragmentation of control over data, analytics, and technology. The CIO or the CDO have, in some cases, ended up creating separate fiefdoms in organizations with their own budgets and promises of driving accountability. Technology challenges are a mess; costs increase, and procurement has to step in again. If your ability to drive return on investment (ROI) is questionable, and you have competitive functions vying for the same budget and procurement as the only unifier, then decisions around marketing are not being made in the interest of the consumer. They are being made as one would toward a necessary but questionably important ingredient in a product.

Marketers in many cases are looking over their shoulders, looking for quick wins that will buy them time and cost control to not run afoul of the CFO. If they get big campaigns or activations wrong, their bosses will read about it in the press. When the economy is uncertain, although it's intuitive that creating demand for your product is crucial for your sales team, most senior leaders prefer to cut budgets with the belief that brands and marketing cannot drive people to buy during a recession. It sort of questions the very premise of marketing itself.

To top it off, CMOs have their jobs made harder by their partners and other parties in this ecosystem.

## PLAYER 2: PLATFORMS

Platforms have replaced most vehicles of marketing and have usurped a giant share of advertising spend, which is a really big component of total marketing spend. And they have constructed an architecture of preferences that has created silos that are beneficial to them. Aided by policy and privacy laws, many of these platforms have become isolated islands. (More on this in the chapters ahead.)

Marketers are left with only two choices: you can choose an open internet without certain preferred inventory, or you could choose preferred inventory without much data coming back in return. Let's break that down a bit. In the first case, as a marketer you get access to engage with audiences on multiple websites or apps where you have the ability to collect data and leverage it to better engage with consumers. For example, you would be able to see that I browsed news around sports and then bought a jersey, thereby letting you know that I am willing to spend on sports. If you're a sports-betting site, that's valuable information for you. But in the walled gardens of Google, Amazon, Apple, or Meta, you get high-quality opportunities to engage with people, but your ability to collect information and use them is limited.

In the end you are faced with a Hobson's choice (two equally unacceptable alternatives). As a marketer, you are really looking to engage your audience, and you're less bothered by the medium or platform that you use to achieve that goal. But you can't really do that when you are presented with a weird rule set that disadvantages you more than helping you succeed.

Social platforms are a different kettle of fish. They are vital to dropping cost per exposure (cost per million impressions or CPMs). And there is enough research behind exposures leading to a positive impact on awareness at the very least. Also, it is great for showing procurement officers and CFOs how you're driving costs down. Social platforms are of course able to achieve this because they present content that is so addictive that people continue to want to engage more. This then leads to content, objectionable or otherwise, getting more airtime than what a society would like. You can see how easily marketing enables some of these practices by pursuing a proxy objective only because the real objective cannot be pursued. Proxies are such a devilish bunch of numbers; they seduce and lead you away from what is truly meaningful. And trust me, proxies populate advertising and marketing.

Platforms hold many of the aces in this colosseum. The only defense they have is that of investment, funding, and expectations. They are expected to produce outlandishly positive results and before we diss them, let's not forget the pension funds and teachers' retirement accounts that are betting on those outlandish returns.

Platforms face scrutiny and criticism of their policies, but they do make a pot of gold as well. Just look at how Meta's earnings bounced back after the Apple privacy changes. (Apple had instituted a new policy that gave consumers a choice on whether they would allow an app to track them or not across other apps or properties owned by other entities. Opt-in rate right now is around 29 percent. That means only one-third of people are OK with allowing apps on their phone to track them. That diminishes the ability of the likes of Meta to understand and profile their users. The less they know about their users, the harder it is to monetize them.)

Cambridge Analytica and Facebook started this whole circus when it came out that information about Facebook users had been obtained and used to profile and manipulate people into voting for specific candidates. The personal information about users was meant to be released for academic purposes and was instead used to drive voting campaigns. As a case, it was bad for marketing and the data industries.

The media and shows like *The Great Hack* drove a narrative that all data-driven marketing was conducted in this fashion. Hate to be the party pooper, but in many cases we in marketing struggle to figure out if we have reached enough people. The question of manipulation is a joke given I can't even tell you how many people watched an ad across platforms without using models or estimations, which could be accurate or wide off the mark.

I couldn't watch more than thirty minutes of *The Great Hack*, I have to admit. It was like eating a dehydrated old chocolate bar that had better chances of breaking your teeth than a well-aimed punch. For a documentary claiming to be about exposing data, I was surprised that they couldn't find the obvious issues and instead focused on dramatizing inaccuracies.

## PLAYER 3: AGENCIES

Agencies across the spectrum (creative, media, PR, health, events, etc.) sit in a very interesting position right at the center of all this chaos. Having been with one agency or the other throughout my twenty-five-year career, I should know. Agencies are the ultimate expression of a conflict of multiple interests. They are primarily aligned to their clients (marketing departments of big companies) but have been one of the victims of marketing being seen as a cost; their fees have taken a hit during the last decade—a result of frequent pitches called by ever-changing CMOs. The faster CMOs turned over, the faster agencies did too. Very few lasting relationships remain. And crazy new words like *floats* and *supply chain finance* have made an appearance. For an industry focused on ideas, it has been shocking to see how they are so undervalued.

And so, agencies have turned their eyes elsewhere: to publishers and technology platforms to make up for the shortfall. I'm not here to defend or object to lack of transparency in media buying or shed light on the topic because others have done so much work on this. The reality though is that agencies are often caught between multiple interests: their own and that of their clients. And increasingly both of those don't align. Their clients are looking for more efficiency (as I mentioned earlier, CMOs are being asked to reduce cost by both CEOs and CFOs since attribution in marketing is sketchy and difficult to achieve). Agencies are therefore looking to cut cost of delivery, but if they did do that by using technology, for example, they get paid less. Since they are getting compensated on the number of people working on a client's business, there is not much incentive to reduce that number. The latest round of the ding-dong battle is around outsourcing. Agencies are looking to outsource repetitive tasks to cheaper destinations; clients want to know where and are of course looking to get the benefit of lower costs.

There are independent agencies and others who are challenging this status quo, but if you are listed on the Street, you have to play the game.

You will see some of the best ideas around marketing on the pitch floor. I'd often joke with my colleagues that if we actually implemented even half of our pitch ideas, the world would be a better place.

## PLAYER 4: MEDIA COMPANIES

I have to say that defining what constitutes a media company is hard. Content creation is no longer a scale-based operation; you as an individual can be a content creator taking the help of a platform that allows your content to be viewed or experienced by a large audience and takes a giant cut out of your earnings or it can be a studio or traditional broadcaster or streamer ... you get my point.

If you are a media company in the traditional sense, you're in for a rollicking time. The relationship between content creation and monetization has never been so muddled by third parties as before. Most publishers in the digital space do not get more than forty cents to the dollar from the ads they carry; the rest goes into various fees and opaque "tech taxes" (hidden margins levied by various providers of sometimes nonessential services).

In India, where I come from, it was common knowledge that if you had a shop on any street, you owed the cops a *hafta* (a weekly payment for their protection). This was also true of gangs; it just depended on who ruled your street at any given point in time. Most publishers would agree that they find themselves in a similar position on the streets of digital town. While supply path optimization (denotes the ability to eliminate intermediaries between advertisers and publishers) is a term that you will hear in many charters, it remains an objective not fully attained. Many mechanisms of a trading marketplace like that of equity, debt, or commodities do not exist in the media marketplace.

The traditional media companies, many of whom have jumped into the "streaming" river, find themselves trying to optimize a mix of subscription, advertising, and merchandise revenues. Some are better and have deeper pockets than others. But even those with big budgets like Netflix have had to open an ad-supported tier.

Media companies have to find a way to monetize content, and this is what most people not in the industry fail to see: you cannot get quality content for free and at some stage you're going to want to watch something other than cats. This relationship between premium content and marketing is wound tight and in its balance lies the future of content and opinions accessible to all.

## PLAYER 5: DATA MANAGEMENT COMPANIES

I have a lot of sympathy for data companies. They are the plumbers of the marketing world. They collect, ingest, categorize, and make available signals that marketers can use to either profile or find or reach valuable audiences. Data companies have two versions: Super Mario and Bowser.

*Super Mario* companies embed privacy in their engineering code, are ethical in making their data collection or use cases. In full transparency as the ex-chief data and marketing technology officer, I was responsible for Acxiom for four years. Acxiom is many things, but probably the best way to describe it is as a data management company that helps empower brands to connect with people. So, I am biased. But such companies do exist, and they do provide information that is useful to many companies. The next time you receive a credit card offer in your mail (the snail type) that seems magically just for you, it's these companies that do most of the work.

And then there are the Bowser companies. These are more prevalent in advertising technology or AdTech. They are far more likely to leverage digital identifiers such as cookies but, in many cases, also use personally identifiable information (PII) to profile people and make them available in digital media buying platforms. Unfortunately, the same methodologies and data sources can be used by hackers, as well as anyone wishing to change political attitudes or spread disinformation.

Most companies have a Jekyll and Hyde mentality: Super Marios in certain cases and Bowsers in others. This is why it's hard to understand many of the issues and why most laws end up trying to stop bad behavior and inflict pain on other law-abiding parties.

There is a belief that data companies traffic in data, sell what they get, and are the principal reason why our privacy is under threat.

There are other players in this colosseum like consultants. But I'm not sure whether they exclusively stay in the colosseum or turn up at the bar as well. Over the last five to six years with opacity increasing in many marketing systems, consultants have proliferated. While they do have an important voice, many of the issues with marketing have not been solved because of them. They can be allies or pests dependent on conditions, but they don't create the problem.

## The Noisy Bar

In the Noisy Bar, there's a lot of chatter, but the noise decibel is too high to hear anything. Everyone's shouting to be heard over the music and crowd—but no one can hear a thing. Who's inside this place and what are their roles?

### PATRON 1: PRIVACY ACTIVISTS

Some of the big legislation coming out of the world of the Noisy Bar includes Europe's General Data Protection Regulation (GDPR) and California Consumer Privacy Act (CCPA). Both are intended as statutes that enhance consumers' data privacy and offer consumer protections. Both stemmed from concerns about privacy, including (especially in Europe) the Cambridge Analytica scandal.

The short version of British consulting company Cambridge Analytica's scandal is that data was collected on Meta (then merely "Facebook") on tens of millions of users without their permission. That data was then used for targeted advertising—including political ads, offering guidance to the campaigns of both Ted Cruz and Donald Trump. Facebook CEO Mark Zuckerberg testified in front of Congress—and apologized. Fines were levied both in the United States and in the United Kingdom. Ultimately, Cambridge Analytica filed for Chapter 7 bankruptcy. I think that if it was any other company, it might have probably died a natural death, but because it was politicians, and it was related to voting, it became a much bigger scandal.

It also spurred legislation on both sides of the pond. In addition, rather than trying to speak to legislation, the advertising and marketing industries have allowed technology platforms to speak on their behalf, in essence, by remaining silent on the issues. The privacy activists have focused their ire on not only companies but also people like Alastair MacWillson, a cybersecurity leader and a founding director of Cambridge Analytica.

We should give credit to privacy activists because without them we would have had a free-for-all, and we would not have had discussions about rights and ethics and the like. I like to believe that marketplaces get better when you have a balanced perspective. Markets require laws and balance.

In fact, I think that some of those laws are going to help sustain marketing because they're going to prevent marketing from indulging in some of its poorer practices like retargeting people. However—and here is the big caveat—I think that marketers should have much more meaningful conversations with privacy activists. In many cases, they are seeking a version of absolutism.

Yes, we want guardrails, but the activists are willfully ignoring the economic impact of many of the policies and legislation that they seek to promote. For example, initial economic costs for California companies for compliance to the CCPA is estimated to amount to $55 billion.[10] It would be naïve to think that those costs are not going to be passed along to consumers. There is nothing in the law that prevents that. I would urge privacy activists to stop demonizing the other side. The Noisy Bar is so loud, no one is having a conversation.

---

10 Aly McDevitt, "CCPA Compliance Costs Projected to Reach $55B," January 10, 202, *Compliance Week*, accessed May 26, 2023, https://www.compliance-week.com/data-privacy/ccpa-compliance-costs-projected-to-reach-55b/27847.article#:~:text=The%20total%20cost%20of%20initial,an%20economic%20impact%20assessment%20report.

I think privacy activists should decide what their objective is. Is your objective to protect the interests of all people? Or is your interest just to protect an ideology? Because if your interest is just to protect an ideology, then there is an economic impact of your policies that goes to the very people you're seeking to protect.

## PATRON 2: REGULATORS AND POLITICIANS

If you question regulators about the impact of their legislation on people and their ability to get jobs, their response is generally along the lines that such concerns are not under their purview. Instead, the economic ministry should be addressing that. Unfortunately, they are on the opposite side of the bar near the band and can't hear a thing.

The governing structures in some of these places are completely wonky. People are reacting to headlines and not really thinking about the type of society they want. And we urgently need to be considering this because the advent of AI on a bigger scale means a few companies are going to control the levers and the rest of us are all going to be dependent on them because they'll become, in essence, too big to fail. A great place to look for this is in the banking industry—where the government has had to step in at different times in history.

I think regulators have listened *too much* to the privacy activists who've listened *too little* to their own people whom they're representing. That's why it's a Noisy Bar. They generate a lot of noise in the headlines, but the reality is the consumer is greatly affected by what happens in the Silent Colosseum. And in those silent arenas today, I do not find enough representatives from the Noisy Bar and vice versa. I put the politicians in this group because regulators are also politically biased and not entirely objective—so the two are bedfellows.

### PATRON 3: INDUSTRY ASSOCIATIONS, CONSULTANTS, AND LOBBYING GROUPS

Industry associations, consultants, and lobbying groups have a big table together in the Noisy Bar. Whether it is the Business Roundtable, Privacy for America, along with the technology giants (who also have a huge lobbying focus), they are all part of the bar. The distinction, though, is that they're all lobbying behind the scenes. They're each trying to get their own interest, but there is no one voice and there is no one public voice. It isn't strong. It doesn't come out with one unified sense of purpose. While there have been independent position papers published, no one has been able to synthesize that and formulate a coherent strategy.

### PATRON 4: THE NEWS MEDIA

All of the Bar Patrons and all of the Players have different talking points and different interests. The news media plays a part, in that with every data scandal, headlines blare. However, we need media that is also willing to do a deep dive into the real issues—and some of those are admittedly "in the weeds." However, we all know news cycles are as rapid as the next trend on X, TikTok, or ratings grabber.

## How Can We Fix It?

We're going to spend time in this book looking at real approaches to solutions. Industry associations can, of course, do a lot of work in this area. But some of the influential companies and their chief executives need to stand up and say, "Enough of this demonization." Imagine if the top-five leaders of corporate America stood up and said, "ESG is very important to us. This is our commitment to cleaning up marketing. But at the same time, this is the value that we add to the economy. This is the number of jobs that we produce. So, let's have a real discussion."

Is advertising or marketing a legitimate use of data? Yes or no? If you answer no, along with the fact that the digital economy is the economy for the future and data is that gasoline that allows the economy to grow, then explain to me: How is the economy going to grow and how are you going to generate jobs?

We are trying to solve the problem of data being used to track, which makes people uncomfortable. But instead of tackling the bigger issues around cyber security and *real* risk, we've picked an easy target, which is marketing. In the next chapter, let's take a look at a fictional company, flesh out the players, and look at what we're up against—and my dream of how to fix it.

# CHAPTER TWO

# How It All (Doesn't) Work(s)

## Ari: The Agency Guy

Ari sat at his desk watching the world go by. It was close to 10:00 p.m., late by office standards, even those of New York. He realized that he was twiddling his thumbs, literally, as he thought about the problem in front of him. Three months ago, his agency had pitched and won the ad business of a low-cost carrier that aspired to break into the ranks of premium airlines. The carrier believed that it was possible to straddle both segments of consumers: premium business-class fare-paying passengers (mostly company executives) and low-cost fare consumers (primarily looking for holidays at the cheapest price).

Ari and his team had presented a strategy that showed it was possible to win in both segments. It relied on the ability to profile the population of the United States using multiple datasets and identify the most valuable consumers in each segment. They had developed personas or profiles of three categories:

- *Wannapreneurs*
- *Holiday Junkies*

- *Low-Fare Mavens*

*Wannapreneurs* were rising entrepreneurs or executives from small and mid-size companies who were looking to grow and did not care much about status and appearances. They were cost-conscious but aspired to better cabin services and were willing to pay a slight premium to afford business-class fares. However, they wouldn't pay full-service business-class fares or their corporate travel policies had strict restrictions.

*Holiday Junkies* were people looking for great vacation deals and packages with discounts if they bought hotel stays, flights, and possibly rented cars through the airline. They were junkies because they took holidays frequently. This included senior citizens who were willing to spend their hard-earned cash and young families who turned up for vacations like clockwork; they were always on the move during school breaks or important family holidays. This was a hard group to crack; it included both the budget traveler as well as luxury travelers, who had many options before them. And competition didn't just include other airlines; it included hotel chains, travel sites, travel aggregators, and credit cards that promised unique rewards and points.

*Low-Fare Mavens* were the regular bread-and-butter travelers or low-cost flyers who were current customers of the airline. They were highly price sensitive and could quickly leave if their expectations were not matched. No amount of luxury or service inducements could compensate them for a higher price. Ari had attached the word *Mavens* to indicate their passion and expertise in hunting for lower prices, but if he were to be honest to himself, also because plain old "low-cost flyers" sounded so lame. He wanted to keep the energy up in the room.

The pitch was over; after multiple rounds of negotiation and repeated meetings, Ari had gotten the airline over the line. He was feted and promoted and found himself with a generous bonus; timing had something to do with that. He had won the business just as appraisal season was on; he couldn't have timed it better himself.

Now came the hard part. He had to deliver. The airline still needed to hit its passenger growth target of 20 percent with specific increases in business-class seats and holiday packages sold. Worse, Ari had pitched assuming they would get the entire spend from the airline group. Turned out that the performance media budget, which was quite sizable and in excess of US$200 million, was managed by an internal team. Performance media were crucial to achieving some of these objectives. They included paid search, social media, and some programmatic media as well. Programmatic media or automated media buying through demand-side platforms (DSPs) and supply-side platforms (SSPs) were split between the internal team and his team. The airline had a direct deal with Google and Meta and were insistent that their internal teams would manage them. The rest of the digital marketplace was left to Ari and his team along with traditional mass media like linear TV, print, audio, etc. Connected TV services like Hulu and Roku were fair game. In other words, the scope of work didn't clearly define ownership.

It would be the Wild West.

The agency's new managing director, Rebecca Stone, had taken the assignment assuming that the airline would be a loss leader—a vital win for the agency to shore up its reputation and scale but a loss-making account for the first two years. Ari was worried that the expected business outcomes did not align with his scope of work, thereby guaranteeing frustration, long nights, and battles galore with the internal team. Rumor had it that the internal team had cautioned the marketing team not to pitch the business since it believed it could handle activation and strategy in-house.

But the internal team sat under the direct sales function and the CMO was loathe to give up control of his budget to another department.

Tomorrow was Day One: Ari's first presentation to the marketing and sales teams. He had two hours to convince them to buy into his segmentation of audiences and the resultant media strategy and to ensure that the creatives that had been presented last week by the creative agency (which did not come from his agency group and was reluctant to partner with his team given that the other agency group had also pitched for the media business and lost) were fully baked into his plan and that partnerships and sponsorships of key properties were in line with the brand's expectations. Finally, he had to ensure that he and his team would not come under withering fire from the internal team, which would see his strategy for the first time.

## Stuart: The Airline's Sales Leader

Stuart was pensive as he went through his morning routines with his six-year-old daughter; even she sensed it. A year ago, he had decided to take the role of running the internal e-sales team at the airline. He had been assured that the airline was on the path of transformation, that multiple functions were being united in a bid to get smarter with winning customers, and that he would have all the levers necessary to effect this change.

Cut to a year later. He had more or less achieved most of the easy changes, but his fight with marketing had persisted. And it now seemed like he had lost. With a new agency coming on board, any chance he had of unifying brand and performance budgets was out the window. It was stupid, in his mind, that the airline continued to see brand advertising and performance advertising as two distinct functions with different objectives. In fact, there wasn't even agreement on the definition of these terms.

Marketing included most digital media as performance channels, whereas Stuart and his team focused on any channel where they could optimize toward sales of tickets or packages. His team had strict goals; there was no room for fluff. They could use any tactic, including bloggers, influencers, TikTok, events, search, affiliate marketing ... the list went on.

They didn't, however, control brand budgets. Marketing could sign big sponsorships, content deals, and spend big budgets on linear TV and look at variables, such as attitudes toward the brand, purchase preferences, and the like. He wasn't quite sure about the goals set for marketing managers; just how were they judged if they couldn't measure final outcomes?

Of course, none of these distinctions mattered in the real world. People just saw it all as advertising and weren't very impressed. Neither his team nor that of marketing could agree on a methodology that could accurately assess the contribution of each channel and tactic to sales. While his team operated on the last click attribution approach, where channels were given credit based on the click that led to a set of actions, such as buying a ticket or package or downloading the airline's app, marketing was left trying to make its case for bigger budgets by developing analytical models that demonstrated the value of brand attitudes in driving behavior changes in people that led to the clicks his team optimized and monitored.

He got the logic; he understood it and accepted the science. He just couldn't control it, however. And in the end, it was a giant fucking mess.

Stuart realized that his daughter was staring at him and had a faint hint of a smile mixed with annoyance etched on her face; he had squeezed toothpaste on his fingers while talking to himself.

## Sarah: The Airline's Research and Analytics Guru

Sarah waited until the B train had slowly made its way through the length of the platform before pushing toward the doors. With multiple accounts of people being pushed onto subway tracks in New York City, she was squeamish in rushing toward an upcoming train. Part of it was also lack of enthusiasm in making her way to work. Today was going to be painful, and a lot of testosterone was going to get spilled over meaningless puffery. She hated it when men got jurisdictional.

But between the agency and the internal e-sales team (what an absolutely silly name in today's age) of the airline, she was going to find herself in the role of arbiter. Running the research and analytics team at the airline was a dream—she and her team were the brains that peered into the interactions between the airline and its customers, both potential and existing; analyzed and determined cause and effect; passed judgment on initiatives; and were sought after in all internal battles. She reported directly to the executive vice president in charge of sales and operations, had the ear of the executive board, and was a trusted confidante to many in senior management. Rumor had it that even the sixty-five-year-old CEO, a veteran of the travel industry, was a fan and went by her numbers.

As the train rattled and rocked its way under the avenues and streets of the city, she couldn't but think of the entire analytics effort as a subway system for the insane. Subway systems were built on the ability to integrate either with other transport systems in the city or between multiple lines so that geography could no longer hinder movement. That was the main principle; it didn't matter where you started in the system, you could get to another node through frequent intersection points that allowed you to hop across the city.

But most marketing analytical systems that had to answer complex questions resembled a subway system that had limited to no intersection points between lines, didn't integrate with other systems, at least not deterministically, and didn't lead to preferred destinations anyway.

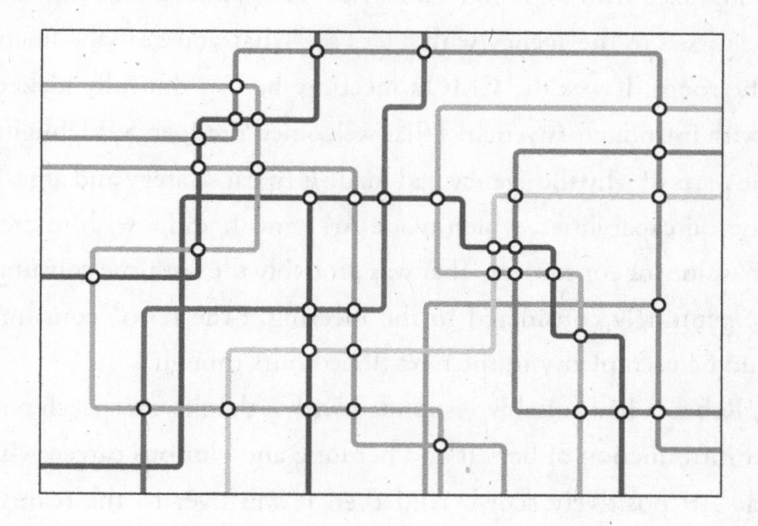

The multiple silos and artificial self-preferencing that dominated the marketing ecosystem made her job really hard, and often she had to rely on smaller models of bigger populations to arrive at conclusions. As media and formats multiplied, as new shiny topics like the metaverse or Web 3.0 came into existence, she found herself struggling to find the right variables to measure and find meaning in the madness.

Having the marketing budget split between multiple departments with no common oversight was a crazy self-inflicted wound that made the madness even more maddening. Now she had to sit in a conference room for three hours and referee the testosterone-fueled landgrabs from marketing, internal e-sales, the new agency, and IT over who did what and who had a bigger you-know-what.

At least she could get to work efficiently.

## The Meeting

It had predictably gone off the rails. The introductions had been cold and sterilized with nods and handshakes all around, a few congratulations tossed to the agency with a let's-see-what-you-got vibe floating in the room. It was the CMO's meeting; he had dutifully kicked it off with introductory remarks that welcomed the agency, highlighted some parts of why the agency had made it (great strategy and amazing analytical capabilities, which made Ari wince), and a wish to create more value for consumers. That was probably the last time consumers were genuinely considered in the meeting. (The term "consumers" would be used plenty in the next three hours though.)

Rebecca had suitably responded with a thank-you speech and a brief introduction of herself and her long and glorious career, which made Ari positively scowl. And then it was over to the teams to introduce themselves with a line about who they were, what they did, and how excited they were to work on the business.

Ari couldn't help but notice that Stuart looked like a fox in the henhouse.

### ROUND ONE

Ari's first ten slides had been a breeze; after all, they referred to information and objectives that were incontrovertible. No one disagreed with what needed to be achieved, and while that seemed minor, there had been enough and more times when a presentation had been derailed on slide five over what an organization was really seeking to achieve.

Slide thirteen was the first point of friction. Ari had started explaining the architecture of the agency's data stack. Every agency had one or was expected to have one. And Ari was lucky in that his agency had actually made investments at the right time and had a stack that was functional and did deliver. Sarah had been impressed with some of the data sources that the agency used and how they had built an API (application programming interface)-friendly platform that allowed for integrations.

Stuart's voice butted into her thoughts.

"I read through your pitch commitments. You mentioned that live feeds could be made available to us if needed; does that include audience data? And if we have built our own audience profiles, can we syndicate them directly to media platforms and bypass your stack altogether?"

Ari's response was measured.

"The live feeds referred to spend and media performance data. We cannot, as yet, give you access to audience data since we are in the process of redoing contracts with data companies. The current contracts allow us to use it for our clients but not to syndicate the data to others. If you have your own profiles, you can load them onto our system, assuming you're using an on-boarder like LiveRamp. If you're using a different on-boarder, then we will have to integrate with the other identity provider and that might take some time."

***Translation:*** *Let me just jump in here—authorial intrusion! No to audience data. It was kind of a stupid question in the first place, more about control rather than real utility value. "I can build a better audience persona than you" was the intended gist. What are audience personas? you ask. They are an attempt to create a profile or view of a single person who is a composite of a section of the population. The single-person persona is supposed to act as the inspiration for media and creative strategies. For example, Jared is single, lives with his mother, goes to the gym, reads no news, is often on TikTok, takes two vacations a year, and is often unhappy with airline baggage fees, which is evident from his Tweets.*

Stuart hadn't intended to come across as a jerk, but he felt the eyes on him as he processed Ari's answer. It was a reasonable one but did beg the question of why the CMO had decided to bring in an external party for data when he and his team could have just as easily done the contracts with the same data providers the agency used and built a stack.

He decided to let it go and nodded his assent as a signal for Ari to proceed.

Ari had barely progressed to mention the utility of taking the airline's customer data and fusing it with the agency data stack when he was cut off again, this time by the CIO of the airline.

"I'm sorry; I thought this was made clear even during the pitch process that we do not share our data with our vendors."

"I remember," Ari responded. "But since the pitch, we have signed a deal with XXX, which is the most secure and robust clean room available in the industry. It's exclusive and an industry first. It will allow us to match our respective datasets without any sharing and allow us to create profiles that allow for better messaging and targeting options. We are not seeking to monetize or profit from your data; we just need to be more accurate in execution."

*Authorial intrusion again: WTF is a data clean room? A data clean room is a secure, protected environment where PII data is anonymized, processed, and stored to be made available for measurement, or data transformations, in a privacy-compliant way. The raw PII is made available to the brand and is only viewable by the brand.*[11]

"Be that as it may, our policy remains unchanged. Proprietary data and customer data is only to be processed, stored, and used by us. We will of course share learnings with you so that you can refine your strategies."

> ***Translation:*** *We will blindfold you and ask you to drive a car but will tell you that there is a cow on the road ahead so you can still steer yourself and us away from it.*

It was maddening but nothing that Ari could do anything about.

He dreaded the next section, on Audiences, and he wasn't wrong: the discussion devolved into a free-for-all over segmentation, look-alike development, sizing, and media pricing.

There was an art to building audience profiles and balancing that with the ability to target profiles through paid media channels. For example, if you picked *Wannapreneurs*, you had to identify the characteristics that defined them and sized the number of such people that you could find across media. It was easier to do so on digital

11 Trevor Testwuide, "What Is a Data Clean Room?" July 12, 2022, accessed October 1, 2023, https://www.measured.com/faq/what-is-a-data-clean-room/.

channels; much harder on traditional media such as TV. And if you mixed the two, that was like finding the Holy Grail. The industry was still seeking such a solution and was far from agreement on standards.

Ari and his analytics team were trying to convince Stuart and his team that the segmentation approach that he had outlined during the pitch could account for the business goals set out but were also findable on media. This involved a fair amount of math and prognostication that neither the CMO nor Sarah was keen on dwelling on.

There needed to be a balance. If the segment was defined very narrowly, you would find very few people in the population. That number may not be sufficient to hit the growth needed or the media cost would be prohibitively high. The elasticity of audience sizes didn't determine the cost of media. They were related, but it was a weak relationship.

The agency had to tread a thin line; be precise but don't lose scale. The airline had to achieve a growth target that was largely set on the basis of competition, analyst expectations, and generalized trends about populations. It broke down when compared to the granular analysis done by Ari and his team. Conversion rates were a given. If there were too few people in the pool to begin with, you wouldn't hit growth. Have too many and you would waste money reaching people who had no intention of getting on your flight.

In the end, the agency's segments were not accepted. Stuart offered Ari a detailed description of the characteristics or signals that the airline identified as important to delineate segments; the CMO was not convinced that the alternatives were any better, and Ari proposed a truce of sorts by agreeing to relook at the segments again.

He sat down with a heavy heart as he handed the meeting over to the strategist. He had done his best to break through some of the issues that had held the airline back in the first place. He also knew that this was just the preamble; they hadn't agreed on who the airline's customers were. As the presentation droned on, people seemed to tune out. The most important elements of strategy were unresolved. Who and how many? And which sources of data were going to be used?

At the end of the meeting, the CMO thanked everyone and outlined next steps, which included getting alignment on the audience and a detailed schematic of the paid media that would run over the next few months. He did, however, give Ari a bit of a win. Stuart was asked to share the e-commerce strategy and his paid media plan with Ari and his team so they could sync their efforts. It left Stuart fuming, but he didn't wish to pick a fight…not just yet.

## TWO MONTHS LATER

Ari, Sarah, and Stuart had decided to meet in the agency to run through the final strategy and plan that was going to be presented to the airline's CEO the next day. They couldn't afford to come across as being disjointed or in each other's faces in front of the airline's top managers. Sarah had played the role of peacekeeper over the last few weeks, gently nudging Stuart and Ari to work together and craft an acceptable approach.

Both men chafed at the idea of making compromises to their goals. But the ecosystem left them with no choice.

The fight over audiences had extended over channels, budget allocation across media, sponsorships, and the final plan. In each case, Ari had to step back and, in some, Stuart just had to accept that he wasn't going to be the point person on big media deals. Sarah had to keep reminding both of them that their tussles had an impact on the measurement plan expected by the airline.

She opened the meeting by trying to summarize what had been agreed and some of the key points that would be discussed the next day.

"On audiences, we are going ahead with the segment names that you originally set out, Ari. But the definitions have been broadened. We have now made *Wannapreneurs* all SMBs, mid-cap company executives, and self-employed professionals. *Holiday Junkies* are those who have taken two vacations or more every year and *Low-fare Mavens* include everyone who has ever flown with us or any other budget airline. Agreed?"

The other two nodded. This had been a painful agreement. The *Wannapreneurs* definition had been diluted; Ari wanted to narrow the base and identify go-getters. He wanted to identify the fastest-growing companies and hit them with a targeted campaign; he didn't want doctors, lawyers, and chartered accountants in the group. They weren't entrepreneurs in his book, but the balance between precision and scale was delicate.

The other two segments had now been broadened; frankly it didn't matter much. Any filters that sharpened the definitions had been dropped in the interests of scale. Also, Stuart was conscious that if he adopted these definitions, his ability to deliver higher returns was impacted. Because in the real world, most valuable consumer definitions did not preclude others from buying.

This was where strategy and the real world collided. The audience definitions used to build the brand and segment users for campaigns would not necessarily translate well in an e-commerce scenario. Anyone who was looking to buy a flight ticket was Stuart's target; he used context and behavior to identify people who were looking to buy.

Ari and his team were incented to look for additional opportunities that would deliver growth. The agency had a performance component in their contract; additional seats sold or packages sold beyond targets would unlock further bonuses. That was, of course, assuming the agency delivered on its cost commitments.

> ***Translation:*** *The whole thing is a fucking mess because multiple departments within a client organization do not necessarily have the same definition of success. Optimization among these various definitions is a tap dance where you step on each other's toes, sometimes deliberately and sometimes with no intention. The other day I was watching my six-year-old learn to play soccer at his weekly class. His friend's father and I would often get very agitated and could be seen directing traffic from the sidelines. On one occasion, my son and his friend were on the same side. Yet, they spent a fair amount of time dribbling the ball away from each other or getting in the way of the other's shot. They were stronger than the other side, taller, older and yet lost 4-0. One of them was a self-goal. Remind you of something?*

Sarah said, "I think we have resolved most issues around the plan itself. Stuart, have you sent details of the paid search plan, the keywords we plan on using, etc., to Ari?"

"Yes, I have. We need to align on our content approach so we use the same keywords in copy and sync up spot schedules so that when TV ads run, we can monitor spikes in search traffic."

Stuart mentioned this as if it was rocket science; it wasn't. The approach had been done for many years now, thought Ari bitterly. The real deal was optimizing across formats: video, short-form content, long-form content, blogs, TikTok, etc. His TikTok deal was done, but it wouldn't involve any performance dollars. And while Stuart would be able to see if TikTok had driven customers to buy packages or tickets, Ari would be blind. He was just the hunting dog that was sent to create noise; the master alone would know whether the hunt was successful.

There were many other issues with the plan, but Sarah didn't want to get entangled in the mess. She knew that both Ari and Stuart were trying to negotiate streaming deals with partners. In the present ecosystem, each partner came with their own measurement partner preferences. And they would inevitably reach out to her to discuss methodologies. It was hilarious if not downright ludicrous. In the days before the plan would launch, both teams would realize that the other had done a deal. The only saving grace was that the partners were different.

***Translation:*** *This happens more commonly than you think. It's called marking your own report card. It works like this. Limit the ability of any third party who has no conflict of interest with either your business or that of the client's to track or measure impact. Privacy of users is a great argument to use. By the way, you have local and national privacy legislation supposedly enacted to defend people's privacy interests to blame. They offer good cover for platforms and any entity to justify not sharing any information with a third party. Once this is done, the only source of information is going to belong to the point of execution. In other words, you get to mark your own report card. Google, Meta, Amazon... they all do it. And now the streaming services are beginning to strike partnerships with their preferred providers to be able to do the same. Of course, this was better than the digital platforms. At least the measurement partners were* *third parties. Imagine if this were true in education. My son could come home with an evaluation from either his favorite teacher or himself. I would have no opportunity to evaluate his performance or his data because it would violate his privacy. He had to consent to allow his data to be accessed by anyone. He could create a marketplace where teachers could compete to conduct evaluations, and he picked the ones that favored him the most. I wished this system existed when I scored steady Cs and Ds in subjects ranging from ****(anonymized to avoid compromising my privacy). If you think this is ridiculous, it is. What's even more ridiculous is when people accuse the marketing and advertising industries of mass manipulation. I often find myself rolling on the floor when I hear about these accusations; more on that later. Do you honestly think Ari, Stuart, and Sarah were scheming or capable of manipulation with their disjointed teams and processes?*

"Lastly, on the measurement plan, we need to align on the reporting that I need to provide to the senior team. Ari, I received your report and dashboard proposal. Stuart, I received yours too. In the interests of sticking to one format, Ari, I'd like you to just either set up feeds for me or send data in Excel sheets. I know it's tedious, but it's the only way I can make these multiple streams work together. I've agreed with my boss that we would only provide monthly reports along with a quarterly summary. Once this meeting gets done tomorrow, we need to set up tiger teams to flesh out the details behind the frequency of data, quality assurance, and making sure we get the right insights from it."

There was no further discussion. The meeting disbanded. It was ironic. Of the thirty minutes planned for the meeting, twenty had been taken up around audiences, five on the plan, and a comment about the measurement plan. The measurement plan was solid: it measured the key performance indicators for the airline: seats booked, revenue from e-commerce, reach of the plan... Wait. Not really. It was the reach of each individual medium or channel with, in some cases, their own measurement partner. And Stuart and Ari used the same media but differently—and sometimes the data did not match.

In short, no one could give a deterministic answer on total people reached, number of times the ad was seen or viewed or shared, etc. There would be islands of sharp clarity and oceans of darkness, which would not be illuminated. Occasionally, one would get to see the most important pieces of the marketing campaign accurately and sharply lit; those would make it to the awards submissions.

***Translation:*** *Ever heard of taxonomy? Or metadata management? Think of taxonomy as a system of classification. Imagine going up to a librarian and asking him or her for a book. The librarian will ask you for the title, author name, publisher, or some identifier, which will allow the librarian to look it up in the system and give you clear directions on where to find it. Data needs the same. You need to know what you have and where it exists. Seems simple enough. But when the volumes increase and discipline lags, you have a swamp. If the library does not follow a standard classification process, the librarian is going to have no idea where to find your book. If Ari's team named a campaign "Wannapreneurs" and Stuart named the same as "Prospects," unless there is an instruction in the system that maps the two names together, they will sit as two discrete entities. Kind of like your wardrobe or at least mine where all the T-shirts never seem to be together, and summer and winter clothes are mixed up. It's always frustrating to find what I want. With data, it just results in incorrect numbers or just plain garbage.*

## The Unhappy Victims: Katherine and Mark

Katharine had just spent the day grading papers of her sixth-grade students. Sixth-grade math seemed to be a challenge for some of her kids, who were largely from struggling households. She worked conscientiously to make sure she was fair in her grading—and that she offered as much extra help as she possibly could to ensure all her students kept up. It had been exhausting work, grading sixty papers once and then reviewing them to make sure she hadn't missed anything.

Katherine was a perfectionist, some would say. She had been in the school for over twenty years and was one of the most respected teachers by both students and her colleagues. Between being the mother of an eighth grader and a fourth grader and a teacher, she had her hands full. Her latest predilection was figuring out how to change the pedagogy given the rise of ChatGPT and other generative AI tools. She didn't agree with her school's approach of banning them; she knew that they had to be integrated into the curriculum. But that was a battle for another day.

Luckily, her husband Mark had decided to work from home for good post the pandemic. He helped her out immensely, taking over household chores, keeping the kitchen running while managing his successful publishing business. He was also involved in the local community and had financial interests in a restaurant chain and had made wise investments that were paying off now.

Theirs was a balanced life. Very different from what they had pre-COVID, but one that they were much happier with.

Although it did come with occasional irritations, all that time at home meant Mark had begun to dominate her Netflix programming choices. Despite multiple suggestions, Mark had not created his own profile, with the result that her profile was awash with zombie flicks and historical war dramas.

She noticed how more time spent by Mark at home meant she received more ads that had nothing to do with her. She received mailers asking her to buy an SUV, lease a new sports car, and travel around the world in a private jet. Mark would wistfully browse and the ads and meaningless messages would follow.

She sighed as she picked up her laptop, ready to jump into her email when she thought of going back to her shopping cart and checking out the books she had wanted to buy for her grade. She was greeted with a full-page takeover from the budget airline yet again, promising to take her on another journey in their new business-class seats to the Caribbean.

She waited for the annoying takeover to minimize before she continued to browse books. An hour later, she moved on to her favorite social networks just to check the photos from last night's dinner that her friend Annalise would have posted. As the page loaded, she watched the airline yet again, this time enticing her to go to the Caribbean but in basic seats that would be really cheap.

She couldn't help but laugh out loud. She was a teacher making 45K a year, and the airline couldn't decide whether she should fly business class or basic coach; whether she was a low-cost flyer or a premium flyer. It just annoyed her, the fact that they didn't know her or her tastes. She didn't want them to know everything about her, but for God's sake, "at least decide what you'd like me to buy!"

****

This case is a composite of many situations and meetings that I have been in or have seen others in. This chapter will be criticized: most will say this doesn't happen in their organizations or that this is an exaggeration. Neither of those criticisms would be true.

The only exaggerations are names and timelines. Usually what I've described would take several months and many meetings to play out. The dysfunction would become visible after the first six months of the honeymoon phase between a new agency and a client. I didn't want to bore you with the six months, hence the compression.

There are many more people, egos, and systems involved than what I have indicated, but the addition of others will not diminish the main point behind the case: marketing and advertising are not able to manipulate or indeed exploit people. Most times, they are trying to keep pace with the changes wrought by technology, data flows, and regulations that assume the worst and are not prepared for the present.

Most marketing ecosystems spend a lot of time assessing the landscape, arriving at the strategy, and deploying a plan. They struggle to make sense of what they can measure. There are three parts to this systemic breakdown: data asymmetry, forced partitioning, and a race to the bottom. One refers to the granularity of data available in the beginning of a campaign and the steady decline of quantum, quality, and dimensionality of signals received from people as the campaign gets into market. The second refers to the measurement inaccuracies that crop up due to the walls set up by large technology platforms that are artificial in nature and are guided by pure self-interest in combination with ill-thought-out legislation that does pretty much the opposite of what it's intended to do.

The third part is what my friend Brian Lesser, CEO of InfoSum and one of the earliest proponents of addressable marketing, terms a race to the bottom. "The mechanism by which you convert customers that already have an awareness your brand has improved manyfold...I think that's come at the expense of building brands and creating new innovative mechanisms to engage your customers. But most of [data and technology] has been applied to below-the-line direct response advertising, which on a P&L is part of the cost of sale, not part of a marketing expense."

If marketers and marketing need to improve people's experiences, if brands need to engage at a meaningful level, and if policymakers are truly interested in creating a fair marketplace where privacy is respected, these are the areas that need the most focus. Therefore, that's where we go next. The next two chapters are the nerdiest and involve taking a journey into the bowels of a ship called marketing. Welcome to chaos…

# CHAPTER THREE

## Fuck If I Know, Part 1

I loved writing this chapter and the next. And because many of you would have groaned on reading the original title, I changed it to a line that accurately describes what this and the next chapter purport to do—show you how f*cked-up the data-driven ecosystem is. (It's not pretty.) In innumerable presentations that I have made, I've faced a unique combination of intense interest and boredom from an audience all at once while discussing these issues. There is a sense that data science and its uneven application in marketing is an important topic, but the jargon, the math, the science, and the gobbledygook make people switch off, get restless, or let their attention wander.

But if there is one piece of advice from me, it would be this: Don't skip this chapter. (Sure, Arun, you're just trying to make us read this book.) Stick with me, and I promise I'll try to make it as easy to understand as possible. Whether you're a senior leader in a marketing organization or a CEO or CFO, you need to know what's in this chapter. If you're a legislator or a policymaker who has picked up this book, this is the chapter you want to bookmark and read before every hearing or policy meeting. If this were a movie, this is where the wheels begin to come off for the hero, there are spectacular misfires and near misses, and a general sense of despair. However, if you don't watch this part, you get no satisfaction in watching the climax.

There is likely to be a fair amount of criticism of this chapter from interested parties, and I'm unlikely to be surprised by that. My objective is to focus on facts, explain concepts, and highlight the dysfunction that pervades the space of data and its applications in the field of marketing. By the time we have traveled through the by-lanes and alleyways of big data, platforms, and silos, you will find more empathy for marketers, with the challenges they face trying to reach people and the abject shit show that has become measurement.

Even if we believe that we understand terms such as *big data*, *identity*, *data brokers*, etc., it's best to refresh our understanding. My attempt here is to not drive too deep into these concepts; just enough to help understand the fundamental paradoxes marketing is beset with. Stick with me because in some of these definitions lie simple truths about how our convoluted understanding of these concepts has exacerbated the mess we find ourselves in.

I enlisted the help of three ex-colleagues to help me get accurate with this and the next chapter for two reasons: one, because they know many of these issues inside out and have been with me in the trenches over the last decade or so, and two, they helped keep me on track and not attempt to boil the ocean.

The trio includes Ian Johnson, former COO of all the data and tech units within IPG and *the* strongest product person I've known. Ian has built platforms, founded start-ups, sold his companies, and most importantly become my right-hand man in navigating a disparate and fragmented advertising and marketing technology landscape.

Another distinguished member is Saqib Mausoof, currently the CDO at Affinity Data Solutions and someone who navigated the complex world of data solutions and activation in an attempt to bridge the gap. He is also the only CDO I am aware of who has a ponytail, talks about crunchies with abandon, and is the guy you want to go hang out with because you're guaranteed to have really fun, engaging conversations on a wide variety of subjects.

The third member is Michael Heberle, who was my chief data scientist at IPG and a person we all relied on to make sense of the madness and get to outcomes that really mattered. He has all the traits of a scientist: a deep understanding of both research and data science, which, let me add, is as hard to get as Indian vegetarian food in Arkansas, and a penchant for being blunt with the truth, a quality I think should be more prized in the worlds of marketing and advertising than it is now.

These three amigos helped me distill some of the concepts and issues that I describe in this chapter.

I also spoke to a number of key people who are driving change for the better, those who have a great understanding of the issues involved and probably have some of the solutions we need to clean up this mess.

## The Rise of Big Data

*Big data* is a term that often gets thrown around a lot, as if it's self-explanatory. There is an automatic assumption that big data is sufficient, scaled, universal, almost like a census but more powerful with answers to any questions we might pose. And in the field of marketing, big data, AI, ML (machine learning), platforms, and tools get used quite a lot, often as if by using these names, universal panaceas have been found.

But the reality is quite different. And before you Google me and check whether I have done any of what I have accused marketing of doing, yes, I have. But as part of getting down from the metaphorical lookout position on the mast, it's important for me to acknowledge that maybe we have used these terms footloose and fancy free and ended up creating an impression of omnipotent insights and activation that is simply not true.

*So, what is big data?*

Let's look at multiple definitions. Most people tend to define big data as datasets that cannot be managed by traditional software and therefore require a completely different branch of computing that helps manage this volume.

And then there are the Vs: Volume, Value, Variety, Veracity (or Fidelity, but then it's not a V!), and Velocity.

- Volume refers to the size of data as is referenced by most definitions of big data.
- Value, which in my mind is the problem and an automatic assumption with big data, refers to the quality of insights that you glean because of looking at patterns that you could otherwise not find with smaller datasets.
- Variety refers to different sources and types of data that you get access to—this is a nod to the ability to connect seemingly disparate datasets and make sense of them.
- Veracity (or fidelity) refers to accuracy of the data—again another element of big data that is often forgotten.
- Velocity is a nod to the speed at which data is collected from the point of generation—and how quickly it becomes usable.

Too much of the conversation around big data is dominated by volume and velocity, whereas if you really want to wring value from your big data investment, you need a variety of sources and veracity as well.

I like to think of big data in terms of rows and columns. In theory, you have a huge number of rows that refer to records and then you have columns that refer to attributes. For example, you could have data of about three hundred million Americans in rows with multiple attributes about them as columns. Attributes refer to descriptors such as age, gender, income, presence of children in the household, political party affiliation, etc.

The devil is in the details though. This setup works best when the data is accurate and deterministic. In other words, ideally you have clarity on the source of the attribute and the accuracy of the information. Deterministic data will use identifiers that can be linked to the record of one of the three hundred million Americans in our example. An identifier could be an email address, a phone number, mobile phone number, an address, a cookie ID, and so on. But importantly, deterministic implies there is a very high chance of it being true.

The other category of data is probabilistic. In this case, the information is inferred or derived. For example, if a cookie ID is observed visiting the Good Housekeeping website multiple times a day, and viewership data from the household shows a number of "women"-related content being watched, you infer that the cookie ID tied to that household belongs to a woman.

However, there is a fair degree of inaccuracy involved. Before I continue, a warning: this is a controversial claim. There will be howls of predictable denials and counterclaims of performance. But in many cases when you have many records and many attributes, to make sure you fill all gaps, various models or probabilistic matches are made. This helps ensure that the data is complete and comparable. It does impact accuracy, though not as much as originally feared.

## Data Artists

I hate the term "data brokers." I don't think that truly encapsulates what companies, such as Acxiom, Epsilon, and others, do. As someone who played a key role in the acquisition of Acxiom for IPG, I know the inherent value of these companies to marketing. But "data brokers" suggests a level of unscrupulous behavior, of trading in assets that don't belong to them. They are used pejoratively, but there is a lot of science and art that goes behind creating the big datasets that don't sit within the walled gardens; hence, I use the term "data artists" to describe them.

They bring a fair amount of value because data in and of itself isn't valuable. Multiple pieces of information need to be stitched together to make sense. The best analogy I can find to explain the concept is found in police procedurals. Imagine the profiler board where detectives write or stick all the information they have found on the case. Over time, they piece events, chronologies, connections between individuals, and patterns of behavior before arriving at the identity of the perpetrator(s).

Creating profiles of individuals or households works similarly. You collect data from multiple sources, public and private, that serve as the raw material before algorithms parse and piece together these disparate indicators into individual or household profiles. It seems easy to describe the process, but to do it at scale, with a high degree of accuracy while being cognizant of privacy laws that govern people from multiple geographic locations, takes skill and discipline to execute.

The known or physical world gives us data about real-world interactions captured through real estate transactions, census, data, etc., while the unknown or digital world gives us cookies, devices, or mobile IDs that come through web browsing, apps, and the like. These two worlds need to be brought together and reconciled because people live in both worlds, and understanding behavior across these worlds is critical. Marketing exists in both dimensions and so do brand experiences—and people expect brand experiences to transfer seamlessly, cohesively, and repeatedly between the two.

Thus, we come to the concept of identity resolution.

## Identity Resolution—How Do I Get to Know You?

Let's begin with Gartner's definition of identity resolution: *It is the discipline of recognizing people across channels and devices and associating them with information used for marketing and advertising.*[12]

In simple terms, it is a means to ensure that an individual, despite their multiple attributes, behaviors, devices, addresses, physical locations, relationships, given and last names, aliases, and phone numbers, gets recognized as one person or as someone belonging to the same household.

When companies such as Acxiom, Epsilon, Experian, Transunion, and the like claim that they have universal datasets that cover the American population, this is what they have done. And when regulators complain about these datasets, they are reacting to the scale and the size of the database without truly understanding the impact these datasets can and should have on marketing. As regulations become more punitive and consent based, these databases are under threat. As the number of data points reduces, the ability of these algorithms to make these connections reduces, the fidelity of the data reduces, and over time the value declines.

12 https://www.gartner.com/en/documents/3902267.

But identity resolution doesn't just end with getting the population identified and classified. They need to be found in the digital world. This is where complexity arises and the diminution of digital signals has a direct impact on the match rate or the number of people you have identified in the real world matched with their digital identifiers or signals such as cookies, browser IDs, email IDs, etc. And these identifiers sit in platforms like Google, Meta, etc.

The transfer to the digital world results in a generational loss. For each person or profile you try to reach on a digital platform, match rates can vary between 40 and 70 percent. In other words, for every one hundred people you can identify in the real world, you might only get forty to seventy of them in the digital world. In some countries like the UK, 20 percent is considered an awesome result. That's twenty out of every one hundred people identified. And this number will keep slipping as more digital signals like cookies get eliminated.

**Katharine and Mark: Blended Identities**

*Returning to the example case of the airline, Katherine's frustrations on being served messages that might have appealed to her husband rather than her arise from the inability to resolve her identity accurately in the digital world. Katherine and Mark have many devices in their home attached to an IP address. If there are no specific signals like sign-in details that can be assigned to Katherine exclusively, then the IP address becomes the default identifier. The browsing behavior across Katherine's and Mark's devices gets blended together with the result that in some identity graph, this household is tagged under one ID. Therefore, the airline cannot differentiate if*

*Mark is looking to book a business flight or Katherine is looking to book a vacation package. The best marketers can do is to spray and pray; it's just more precise than twenty years ago when folks were carpet bombed with messages on linear TV. But it's not the precise rocket science that it's made out to be. And we have only looked at the effort involved in being able to profile people and target them on media. ("Target" is a term that I dislike immensely because it conjures visions of precision, which isn't accurate but it's the term most widely used in the industry and I decided to let it be. It is important to note that the word triggers negative reactions from people and regulators not in the marketing industry.)*

Prior to big data, panels and primary research were the only mechanisms to understand behaviors or track impact. Panels recruited people who fit the audience profile needed and provided longitudinal data repeatedly over a period of time to enable consistent reporting of behaviors and impact. It's what the likes of Nielsen do in measuring ad exposures, brand lift studies, recall, etc., and despite all the brouhaha over big data it still remains a universally accepted approach for both profiling and measurement. The first Nielsen TV ratings system based on panel data began in 1950.

With panels and surveys, we had fewer rows representing the population and a number of different columns that were broadly descriptive of the audience. It took time to do the math to project the data on the entire population and was in many cases slower to be made available. It wasn't real time and was akin to looking at snapshots over time of people and events. In some cases, it could mimic movement because you had a number of snapshots taken in close succession. The one advantage of these snapshots was resolution. Depending on the variables that were most important in a situation, the depth of information could be varied. Today big datasets offer video but, unlike most assumptions, the resolution is not uniform. They resemble a buffering video, which is often pixelated. In some cases, you could see that static pictures had been co-opted into creating an impression of movement.

Most of us can recall the sequence from *The Matrix Reloaded* where Neo fights multiple Agent Smiths. As *The New York Times* described in an article in 2003, "When the action became dangerous, stunt doubles were used. If the stuntman was far from the camera, he was simply dressed like Agent Smith; if the action was closer, the stuntman's head was digitally replaced by that of a virtual Smith. When the action became unrealistic, as in the sequence in which Neo swings around a pole at warp speed to attack the advancing Smith clones, the entire scene—actors, sets, camera movement, and lighting—was created on the computer."[13]

This acts as a good analogy to the way big datasets deal with complex populations. There is inherently no weakness in the approach but it's essential to understand that certain parts of the information are "created" through inference and fusion with panel data, and some of the connections made between attributes of an individual or a household are tenuous and not as accurate as is made out.

I had a chat with Scott McKinley, the CEO of Truthset, a company that validates data, and some of his stats were astounding. Apparently, IP addresses are only 40 percent accurate in identify-

13 Eric A. Taub, "The Matrix Invented: A World of Special Effects," *The New York Times*, June 3, 2003, accessed July 28, 2023, https://www.nytimes.com/2003/06/03/business/the-matrix-invented-a-world-of-special-effects.html.

ing households and addresses. Tying the correct email address to the correct postal address is done accurately about 51 percent of the time by big data vendors. Truthset has just formed the Data Collective, an initiative that focuses on driving data accuracy and one that I think the industry needs more than ever.

Way before big data became a thing for marketing, in a paper published in the *National Science Review* in June 2014, the authors talked about the issues facing big data analysis: "massive sample size, and high dimensionality bring heterogeneity, noise accumulation, spurious correlation, and incidental endogeneity."[14]

In plain English, when you have a high sample size and a large number of attributes that arise from unifying multiple sources of information, you end up with the promise that you can identify even weak common signals from populations. But you also end up with correlations that seem causal but are not; the sample sizes are so large that even random variables end up having correlations, in some cases unintentionally so. The paper does an excellent job of explaining this: "Unlike spurious correlation, incidental endogeneity refers to the genuine existence of correlations between variables unintentionally, both due to high dimensionality. The former is analogous to find two persons look alike but have no genetic relation, whereas the latter is similar to bumping into an acquaintance, both easily occurring in a big city."[15]

As more signals from people get turned off, re-creations and simulations will only increase.

This is the source data for how audiences are created, profiled, and syndicated across the media and marketing worlds.

---

14 Jianqing Fan, Fang Han, Han Liu, "Challenges of Big Data Analysis," *National Science Review* 1, no. 2 (June 2014): 293-314, accessed July 27, 2023, https://academic.oup.com/nsr/article/1/2/293/1397586.

15 Ibid.

## It's All About the Audience, Stupid

"Audience" is a media word coined to describe people passively engaging with a piece of content. It's often used to describe targets or recipients of marketing communication. But businesses don't think of audiences; they think of consumers, existing and potential, new to category or new to brand, budget-conscious or premium, located in cities and/or suburbs...the list goes on.

The science and art of identifying the right audiences is in effect a battleground for dueling strategies, sometimes at an enterprise level. (I'm keeping with the existing marketing semantics and using the term "audience" still because it's hard for me to change my own vocabulary after twenty-five years of chanting the name.) Some of the choices outlined here can essentially impact distribution and pricing strategies, brand portfolio management, identification of gaps in the market, and so on. Each of these is a big strategic choice to be made by a business, which is why I always get excited when talking about audience creation.

When I was a media director on the P&G business in China back in 2005, I used to love going on tours with P&G brand managers. We used to hit the road and wind our way through a province, speaking to retailers, seeing how consumers bought our products, assessing shelf domination, and getting real feedback on my media plans. I never knew what I was going to hear, and some of what I heard surprised me. The biggest surprises were mostly regarding audience definitions, behaviors, and characteristics of people we thought we knew because we had pored through multiple reams of panel and survey data—and yet we had gotten wrong.

Keep in mind that today's audience definitions are being crafted based on some of the big datasets that are voluminous and have a reasonably good refresh rate, but hide deficiencies that get amplified when deployed at scale.

This is the beginning of the journey of asymmetry, a slow slide in volume, type, and value as we progress through the marketing process.

## Audience Creation

At the heart of creating audiences lies familiar questions: Who are my buyers? Who do I need to influence? How deep in the population do I need to go to achieve my business goals? These seem simple, and a lot of marketing is, but some fundamental changes in the way we have chosen to answer these questions, led by promises of hypertargeting and cheaper exposures, have in my mind led to many of the challenges marketing faces today and in the future.

Tom Denford is the CEO and founder of the ID Comms Group, a media consultancy group that helps brand and marketing teams identify the right media agency partners or, in other words, a pitch consultant. But since I've worked with Tom in my past life at Aegis, I recognized a deep strategic bent of mind and a willingness to change the status quo in him. Over the years, Tom has been one of the key voices urging a clean-up and refocusing of the industry on what matters: brands and helping brands win the marketplace. When I spoke to him, one of the first papers he shared with me was about good old basic media principles. In July 2015, the Ehrenberg-Bass Institute for Marketing Science in the University of Southern Australia issued Report 66, a primer on best practice media principles that had research over the last forty years backing them. These principles were written with an objective to make brands grow. Granted, the report is dated and many improvements in data collection and analytics have occurred in the last five years, but the principles espoused by the report still serve as a good contrast to some of the beliefs driving today's tactics. Caveat: In a later chapter, I will illustrate how some of the old models don't quite capture the needs of marketing today. The basics still work, but some of the thinking needs to and has evolved.

I found it quite refreshing to read the report; it took me back to basic marketing principles, and I was quite shocked at how far I had come along from some of the precepts I had studied and accepted years ago.

The first principle in the report talks about targeting the market: "Media investment should aim to reach all category buyers, from the very heaviest to the very lightest." It adds: "Traditional marketing theory encourages skewing spend toward the brand's most frequent buyers, or heaviest category buyers ('golden households' or 'super consumers'); however, this is not a growth strategy. Reaching light buyers is essential for both brand maintenance and growth."

On the face of it, there is nothing in this principle that seems counterintuitive, but it has fundamental implications on a media plan where a giant part of marketing investment sits. High-reach media becomes an automatic choice and, as per the paper, "Many media options look attractive because they claim 'low wastage'; heavier buyers of the category (or even just buyers of the brand!). This can be much less attractive than it sounds because such buyers are often the easiest to reach with any media."

In 2010, I first came across the concept of programmatic media buying. To be quite honest, for all my current claims of being a visionary, I struggled with accepting the basis or the promise that lay in being able to differentiate and engage people differently based on their importance to the brand and to do so at scale. In other words, you could value the light buyers of the category or brand differently and pay a premium to reach them while limiting your exposure to heavier buyers. And you could do this by being precise, and automation would ensure that this could be done at scale.

There doesn't seem to be any contradiction between the promises of programmatic media buying (or addressable buying, which I prefer) and the principle outlined by Ehrenberg-Bass. But there were two fundamental assumptions embedded in the promise of addressable buying: One, data would let us identify light buyers or buyers of other brands, and two, *this data, without losing its accuracy or character, would be available to us at the time of planning, execution, and measurement.*

Most audience identification approaches today follow the promises made by programmatic media a decade ago, but the second assumption has proven to be a pipe dream with the result that frequently the principle of Ehrenberg-Bass gets violated more than followed in practice.

A modern-day audience identification process looks like the following.

## The Art of Audience Creation

Even though a fair amount of math is involved, I've deliberately used the word *art* to describe the audience creation process. Once you go through it, you'll probably realize, like me, that there are so many qualitative and quantitative judgments that get made that affect the outcome. And no matter how senior you are, I urge you to dive into the details. Too many people with influential decision-making powers do not dive into this mess, and I can see why, but I plan on dragging you through this mesh of interconnected decisions if nothing but for my own pleasure but also because the next time you sit in a presentation and someone like me tries to awe you with a data-driven approach, you will ask the right questions and make the right trade-offs.

As a side note, while being "creative" with data is not encouraged, I find this process no less exciting than creating a thirty-second spot.

The first step begins with the creation of seed data. Seed data can come from two sources: either the brand's own customer list (or first-party data as it is commonly referred to) or third-party data, which is data that you tend to buy to help profile a potential audience. Even if you're a brand that is lucky to have a fair amount of information about your customers, it will in most cases be a fraction of the total population. For our purposes, I'm describing this process for the United States, but it remains the same for other markets; the only distinction lies in the third-party information available to buy.

The idea behind creating seed data is to have a starting point. If you have existing customer data, you begin with them or their profiles. In some cases, you might begin from existing customer segmentation. With first-party data, you may have limited fields; you may not know customer addresses or phone numbers or might only have emails.

In the case of segmentation, there is primary research that has created aggregated groups or segments of the population identifying those most valuable for growth or profit.

## The Audience Chart

| First-Party Data | CDP/DMP | LAL (Lookalike Models) | ID Match | Demand-Side Platform (DSP) | Platform LAL + Ad Exposure |
|---|---|---|---|---|---|
| 20K Records | +30K Cookie IDs / MAIDs | +Clean Rooms/US Data Spine | Digital IDs | Cookies (x2) | 2x Day / 5x Week Frequency |
| Total: 20K | Total: 50K | Total: 500K | Total: 350K | Total: 700K | Total: 15 million |

1,500 Users

7 Million Ad Exposures Tracked

For the purposes of this discussion, assume we managed to find records of twenty thousand individual consumers from the airline's database. As usually happens in large organizations, CRM systems are used concurrently with customer data platforms (CDPs) and/or data management platforms (DMPs). There will in all likelihood also be a web analytics product involved, such as Adobe Analytics, which would probably feed these systems. Adobe has a suite of products, which might help prevent data transfer loss. These systems capture information from digital behavior in the form of cookies or mobile ad IDs (MAIDs). Assuming that some of these records are unique with no overlap with other CRM systems in the organization, we add another thirty thousand identifiers to the mix.

We have twenty thousand records with PII and thirty thousand digital identifier records that have no PII attached. I'm not using legal definitions utilized in privacy laws; if you believe most privacy laws like the European GDPR, any identifier is personally identifiable, but I'd like to make the distinction between knowing your cookie ID versus knowing your home address. Maybe I'm trying to hide behind common sense, but cookies have become a convenient target for all involved with vested interests.

As a next step, we have to flesh out these fifty thousand records and fill gaps in the information.

This is where big datasets such as Acxiom's Infobase, Experian, Epsilon, Transunion, or Neustar step in. They have what is called a US data spine. If Ari had received permission to get access to the airline's data in the previous chapter, this is what he and his team would have probably done.

They would have taken the airline customer data and fused it with that of a big data provider. Wait…let's stop a second. I feel like I'm back to my sales spiel trying to sell my big data wares. Let's unpack what *fusion* means.

Let's assume I'm in the customer database. The airline might have my name, phone number, and email address along with my address and credit card information. It has my travel history, seat and meal preferences, and maybe other household members' information if I have signed up for their rewards program and share them with other family members. But it wouldn't know that I had just purchased an SUV or that I have a sound credit history; it won't have my income data or any other email or physical addresses I use or have used. Big data providers do and the connect point is usually a physical address or an email address or a mobile number. I might have given my name differently in three different places, but with an airline, I would give my legal name and a billing address that probably matches my residential address. The airline's record of my physical address could help tie all the other information that a big data provider knows about that address to my customer record.

There is also an ability to take digital identifiers such as cookies and MAIDs collected from the airline's website or app and match back to the US data spine.

The airline now knows a lot more about me. And because it knows more attributes, there is a greater chance of finding me in more databases. Here arrives the first problem with data-driven marketing: it depends on volume for making connections. The airline will never use my auto-purchase record for any benefit; after all, if you have my household income data, you will get a pretty good estimate of my wealth. Add that to the travel history the airline already has and Bob's your uncle. The only way the auto-purchase record might help is if in some database I'm tagged as an auto intender or interested in autos and am using a set of credentials the airline does not have, then this allows them to make the connection and thereby increases the chances of finding me in any digital media platform. Because the links are made by overlapping pieces of information, databases need information that is duplicative across many of them.

If you want to benefit from this economy, the more attributes you store and connect, the greater the chances of finding people and monetizing them. Before I jump into a wormhole, let's pause and acknowledge that this is such a different approach to understanding populations. The fundamental thesis of research is that you can, with a great degree of accuracy, identify people, their interests, and the places they are likely to be found by studying a small subset of the population that is statistically significant in great detail: in other words, a few rows and many columns.

The modern audience identification approach upends that. More is a requirement.

Let's get back to the seed. Ari finally managed to get all fifty thousand customers of the airline profiled. That's still not a significant number though.

The traditional media model has always relied on reach being the fundamental metric of delivery. I can get you more of the people you need: "people you need" being defined very broadly. As we go through this process, keep it in mind. Because by identifying future customers as look-alikes of present customers, we are dangerously close to violating that rule.

You could argue that using a broad-based segmentation would help, but even in that process you are trying to whittle down the number of people in the segments. That's the process of hyper-segmentation.

Enter the oft-abused and misunderstood look-alike models.

When it comes to scaling smaller audience sets, however, mix art, a bit of ethical corruption, and a healthy dose of opacity, and you have the beginnings of a precision campaign going wrong. Before we jump into look-alike modeling, let me answer the question that may be in your head: Isn't this guy in some shape or form also responsible for this? The answer unequivocally is yes. It's also the reason why being smart with the trees does not translate to being smart with forests.

Look-alike models are a standard data science practice: any data scientist would know about them, and most of us probably use them anyway. But it's easy to look at the simple nomenclature and not dive too deep.

These models can be derived in many ways. A generic way is to use the US data spine and find others who are similar to the seed audience created. Instead of getting into the detailed gobbledygook process of how this is done (I was not a fan of math class in school), I'll summarize. In short, you use feature engineering, a machine-learning mechanism of extracting features from raw data. And you do this to identify variables or features on which you can run training or propensity models to arrive at the ones that sharply define the audience.

For example, income, age, and gender might be the main variables that impact travel product purchase. You might also come up with variables that are intuitively correct but that don't pop up first on any list: for example, the presence of children in the household or recently moved from a city to a suburb or bought a new home, all indicators of lifestyle changes or increases in income.

Another way is to split the seed data into two halves; one ends up providing the training data and the other serves as data for validation. In simple terms, use one-half to predict the other, and you get a model that is accurate. Again, since it trains on data that you have from existing consumers or some potential prospects, there is a very good chance that it doesn't reflect the true size of the opportunity. You take the resulting model and deploy it on the total population to arrive at a scaled audience that looks like the seed. In our case study, Ari has scaled the audience of fifty thousand consumers to five hundred thousand potentials by using look-alike modeling with the US data spine. These five hundred thousand individuals need to be found on media platforms for Ari and his team to buy ad inventory against.

For the purposes of this example, I'm going to use one of the simplest and supposedly most effective use cases: reaching consumers through addressable or programmatic media. In other words, I am not exploring media, such as old-school linear TV, or newfangled media, such as connected TV. It doesn't mean we don't want to replicate this process on those media; it's just easier to do it through programmatic media, and this is where it all started anyway.

Onboarding is the ability to tie these people for whom Ari has PII and some digital information into the cookie and MAID world of platforms like Meta, Google, or other independents such as The Trade Desk. There are many ways of doing this, but again I'm going to look at the default option of using an on-boarder, such as Ramp.

Providers like Ramp have created the digital version of the US data spine tying billions of cookies and MAIDs to individuals and households. When onboarding, the first thing to realize is that you're not going to find a match for all the five hundred thousand individuals you have. For a variety of reasons, including the data collected, the recency of the cookies that have been tagged and mapped to individuals or households, and the fact that the Open Web today does not have the greatest share of traffic, there is a drop. I'm going to assume a 70 percent match rate, which is quite healthy.

Ari, post onboarding, has managed to find digital IDs for 350,000 customers, a 30 percent loss in fidelity.

Onboarded to what? you ask. Again, to keep it simple, let's say he is using only one DSP to run the campaign. DSPs are automated platforms that allow buyers to find audiences in various inventory sources and bid for them. There are also other mechanisms of trading. There is no part of this that is simple and not convoluted, and I'm desperately trying to keep us all on track. So, if you find this simplistic, then apologies, but the points I will make at the end of this will not be lost due to the simplification. They are hidden in plain sight.

In this DSP or platform, Ari onboarded 350,000 IDs and has also managed to connect them to 700,000 cookies. Each individual has multiple devices and cookies attached to them; I've deliberately kept the number small.

Now we have 700,000 identifiers. That doesn't translate to enough ad exposures. Of course, some of this is tied to campaign objectives and goals to be achieved, but given media works at scale, even with smaller assumptions there will be a further expansion of this audience.

Back to our friend, look-alike modeling or LAL. We can repeat the LAL process within the DSP or other sources of inventory, like publishers. Being conservative, assume the 700,000 identifiers expanded to 1.5 million. We have now used LALs two times in the process.

There is some ethical corruption involved though. When look-alike models get built, a critical factor is the percentage of population that you would like the model to find. For example, let's say that Ari's audience is largely young women who drive Subarus and have incomes greater than $100,000 per year. A strict like-for-like might produce a pool of 5 percent of the population. But if you want to buy more media against audiences, you could relax the requirement: Your look-alike might just include young women. That might increase the percentage of population covered to be 30 percent; that would justify the marketing budget and the staff on the account and the resulting fees, etc. Here is the second problem with data-driven marketing:

look-alikes may look alike, but they are not the same. And in so many discussions, look-alike models get thrown around as if their very mention should mean rigor and robustness.

Just to mess with your heads, let me add that a number of data providers create propensity or look-alike models based on their datasets in order to cover 100 percent of the population. So…er… that means in some cases we have built a look-alike on a look-alike to be matched into a world with some real people and some look-alikes.

To shed more light on this topic, I'd recommend reading *Big Data in Market Research: Why More Data Does Not Automatically Mean Better Information* by Volker Bosch that was published in 2016 in *Marketing & Data Science.* As the author says:

> *"Even if almost the whole population is reached, like in a census, critical information is missing, such as sociodemographic data. Therefore, the value of the collected data is limited and important evaluations such as target group or segment-specific analyses cannot be conducted. The missing information can only be filled in using statistical data imputation. [Another word for LAL] This requires an additional data source with the additional variables, for example a panel. The source must also contain the variables of the big data dataset. Imputation is a statistical procedure that is anything but trivial."*

As I wrote about this, I instinctively ducked under my table. I could just see so many stones heading my way from various interested parties who would accuse me of total ignorance on such matters and vocally defend their complete dedication to accuracy.

I'm not denying some of my ignorance, but this issue is not about anyone's complicity. It is about feeding a beast, and while I'm not questioning the integrity of individual organizations, I am questioning our collective commitment to this industry we love. And how is it not apparent to us that this methodology cannot be used to describe precision? Using a sniper rifle in a close combat situation does not imply that you're a sniper; it probably means you're going to die quickly.

Getting back to the 1.5 million identifiers we have in the platform, all unique, let's get to actual exposures. Assuming each of these 1.5 million saw the ad twice a day for five days a week, that's 15 million exposures in a week. Let's stop here before the numbers start ballooning up.

This last step is critical; it's what CMOs and media teams need in order to justify their spend, as well as quantify impact. We want to be able to take the exposures and tie them back to the individual audiences and then check whether, as a result of this messaging, there was any movement in flights or packages booked.

In the end if Ari is lucky, he will probably get about 1,500 conversions on the airline site in terms of packages and/or flights sold. There is, of course, the possibility that some of these 1,500 conversions were influenced by more than advertising, for example, word of mouth, but there is no way of telling in the granular detail.

He would also be lucky to attribute 50 percent of ad exposures to individuals. Between the deliberate obfuscation of platforms in sending back information and aggregating data across clusters or cohorts, we can only know what roughly 50 percent of the exposures achieved.

Replicate this across multiple digital platforms, and the numbers worsen. As cross-device measurement gets stifled by platforms camouflaging themselves as privacy activists, frequency goes missing. Ari will have no idea how many times Katherine saw the ad. Or how frustrated she would become having watched the damn thing forty times while bingeing a show on a streaming platform. And if Katherine does buy a ticket, God help her, Ari has a 50 percent chance of knowing she actually did that. And, therefore, there is a 50 percent chance that she will continue to be reminded to book the flight.

*Half the money I spend on advertising is wasted; the trouble is I don't know which half.* John Wanamaker supposedly gave this oft-repeated quote more than a hundred years ago. And my data and digital brethren are still trying to prove him wrong.

We may be able to tell you a lot more about what got wasted and in some very limited cases, even give you the full picture. The bigger the advertiser that you are, the more likely that you are going to rely on modeling and projections to assume truth than know what really drives success. And the bigger and more fragmented you are, the more likely you are to be frustrating your consumers.

As Jack Myers, media ecologist and founder of Media Village, a resource for market intelligence in our industry, says, "While there's targeting, more targeting perhaps...nonetheless a lot of the buying still seems to come back to age, gender, traditional metrics, and currency models."

There are, of course, solutions to these problems. Market mix models (MMMs) based on econometric approaches can, with the right datasets and diligent discipline, identify certain causal connections between events. They can predict outcomes and outline reasons for success or failure. But these models would come later in time, long after campaigns have finished execution and would be great to inform the future rather than influence the present.

Tying macro variables or outcomes like sales, brand, or purchase lifts, etc., to media variables like CPMs or viewability scores is tough.

It again requires leading indicator models built over time that are bespoke to clients, tied into activation platforms to keep an eye on the future while driving in the present.

As an example, Michael Heberle cites the case of COVID-19 death attribution. There was a fair amount of debate over the impact of COVID on death rates and whether it indeed was as much a killer as originally feared. When patients had preexisting conditions, did they die because they caught COVID or did they die because of their preexisting health conditions, such as heart disease, cancer, etc.? Politics made answering the question harder. Even though there was individual-level data being collected, it had all the inaccuracies, gaps, and delays that mimic some of the data collection involved in marketing.

The solution was aggregate modeling.

Michael noted that we can look at death rates by country—and access *years* of data that was counted fairly accurately, or very accurately. We thus know the average rate of death of the population we are examining. Then we can examine the death rate over the course of the global pandemic. With the right factors being considered, we can arrive at an estimation of the excess death rate. All of a sudden, you have a very clean picture as to the magnitude of the impact of COVID. But, as Michael stated in our interview, "This is interestingly only revealed once you use aggregate modeling techniques. … I'm comparing my actuals versus the baseline. That's all I'm doing. And I know 'something' [pandemic] happened."

It brings us to a topic that I both loved and dreaded in school: research and statistics.

## The Decline of Research

When I first joined the industry in India in 1998, there was one maxim that you ignored at your peril: research was king. You had to get your facts right; methodology mattered; and sample sizes, biases, and accuracy determined your path. My mentor, V. Ramani, ex-head of MPG India, a man who was one of the first people to help scale digital advertising in India, was always on my case with numbers.

We used to pore through readership surveys, develop reach curves for multiple media, and try to identify audiences and markets through multiple pieces of research, solving for low sample sizes in rural India, which was ironic, given a majority of India is still classified as rural. Those were heady times.

I used to keep a wardrobe in my office and wouldn't go home for days, living out of the office, preparing go-to-market reports for companies that had asked for media plans.

I still cannot forget the expression on the face of a CMO of a large Indian bank, who had called for a media pitch to choose an agency to help manage his media investments. We gave him a book, close to a hundred pages of analysis, challenging his market prioritization in the brief. We didn't win, but I did catch the bug for research, the science behind it, and the creativity needed to frame a problem.

Like Ramani, who sadly passed away more than a decade ago, research seems to have passed from the limelight as well. Data science has taken over without some of the rigor and discipline that underlined research. When you have plenty, you tend to overlook that which you don't have. And in the case of data, it tends to be the attributes that have been inferred or filled in without an accurate representation of the population.

Michael spoke to me about the rigor involved when he worked at IRI and Nielsen. "We had a whole measurement science team that would do nothing but try to figure out how to do better sampling. How do you stratify the sample? Some of that art has gone by the wayside. Because a lot of the folks that know that kind of stuff are now dismissed as tinkerers. They're a little removed from the actual business outcomes and/or creation of marketing. They're not considered relevant in the conversation."

Dr. Radha Subramanyam, EVP chief research and analytics officer for CBS and president of CBS Vision, said as much, as well. Sitting in her corner office in Times Square, we talked about the unfortunate decline of research in a data-driven world.

She told me, "The problem is a lot of researchers have been substituted with data analysts who don't have a research background. So, they may know how to write SQL queries, or they may know which Python module to use, but they have not been trained in the rigor of statistics."

What's the solution?

In Radha's viewpoint, "The new CDO or chief research officer has to be both traditionally trained, and have a deep understanding of big data and algorithms. If you come up through pure data science ranks, you know how to write code, but you have no sense of what it means. If you are a pure researcher, which I, by the way, really value, you're gonna have to learn how to write some code. So, the leaders of the future, but also the *teams* of the future, have to be 100 percent hybrid in skills."

I asked Michael, who has built many audiences and wrestled with many of the models that needed to be built, a simple question: On a scale of one to ten, where one is spray and pray and ten is hyper-targeted and precise, on average where do we rank? Keep in mind that the industry is quite a broad term; it includes brands that have reliable first-party data and others that don't. I asked him this question while keeping out the brands that come with large datasets because of the businesses they are in. His answer nevertheless shocked me: he'd give us a two or three. In other words, not much better than spray and pray.

Again, there are conditions where you could score a ten. If all you did was take your customer list, match it into Facebook, and run a campaign within the walls of Meta, that's probably a ten. But that's not what most brands do.

Even within Meta, as Michael explains, you're likely to get aggregate information back but not granular information about individuals, even if they came from a brand's dataset. Facebook might have the ability to study the data but not the marketer. And most platforms cite privacy as the reason why they cannot share information with other platforms—and their second message is "Trust Us."

In order to do a sense check, I talked to a few marketers on whether they believed in the audience build process and the general prevalence of data.

Andrea Brimmer, CMO of Ally Financial, had a balanced take. "I think we have made progress in terms of truly understanding the consumer and being better at delivering more precise and addressable audiences. On behalf of brands, I'm not certain that we have completed the loop, which is adding value to the consumer."

Bob Liodice of the ANA (Association of National Advertisers), which represents the marketing community of the United States, is blunt: "Even though we're swimming in data, marketers probably don't have half of the data they absolutely need to make the most effective decisions."

## So What the Fuck Did We Just Go Through?

A lot. There is a lot more to come; we're in the middle of the cave. There is no turning back now; you have to stick with me.

But a quick summary is in order.

*Lesson One:* Big data is large datasets that need computing power to analyze. I think of them as a large number of rows and columns—in other words, attribute information about large populations. Most folks are focused on volume of data and the speed at which it can be collected, processed, and made available to use. Less attention is given to veracity because that is assumed. Don't do that.

To understand people, the industry depends on data artists, not brokers, to bring together physical world data. And then we need to merge that with digital data. These datasets are different, both in volume and fidelity. Identity resolution is hard, and there is a generational loss while trying to make the connection between the physical and digital worlds. Still a struggle to understand?

*Task One:* Watch *Matrix Reloaded* scenes where Neo fights a hundred Smiths. The way those scenes are shot is the way big data gets fused together. (Plus, who doesn't want to rewatch Keanu Reeves being a badass?)

*Task Two:* Read up on basic principles of marketing and media.

Audience creation is complex and fundamentally differs from the aforementioned principles. Audiences are built to identify those who are most likely to receive a brand's message or buy a product; most techniques of audience creation, however, involve scaling narrow audiences. The process of scaling requires building look-alike models in most cases.

*Lesson Two:* Look-alike models simulate seed audiences, but that doesn't mean they are accurate or representative in all cases.

*Task Three:* In the next meeting you have around data-driven marketing, anyone who uses the term "look-alike models" needs to put five dollars in the LAL swear jar. (Fair play!)

Read the Audience Creation and Syndication chart mentioned earlier; it's a good reminder of what can be achieved.

Respect the role of research and identify the level at which you want to seek answers: sometimes aggregate models done with rigor can give you answers that big data models powered by individual data cannot.

While we outlined a simple use case of syndicating audiences to a platform for activation, one of the elements we slid past was the role platforms play in the collection or non-collection of data. And while we have extensively focused on paid media, there is an entire world of CRM, marketing clouds, and other platforms that purports to connect marketing to other parts of an enterprise and make it better, which we need to understand. Data flows are one part of the story; your favorite platforms are the other part.

The Fuck-if-I-Know show continues.

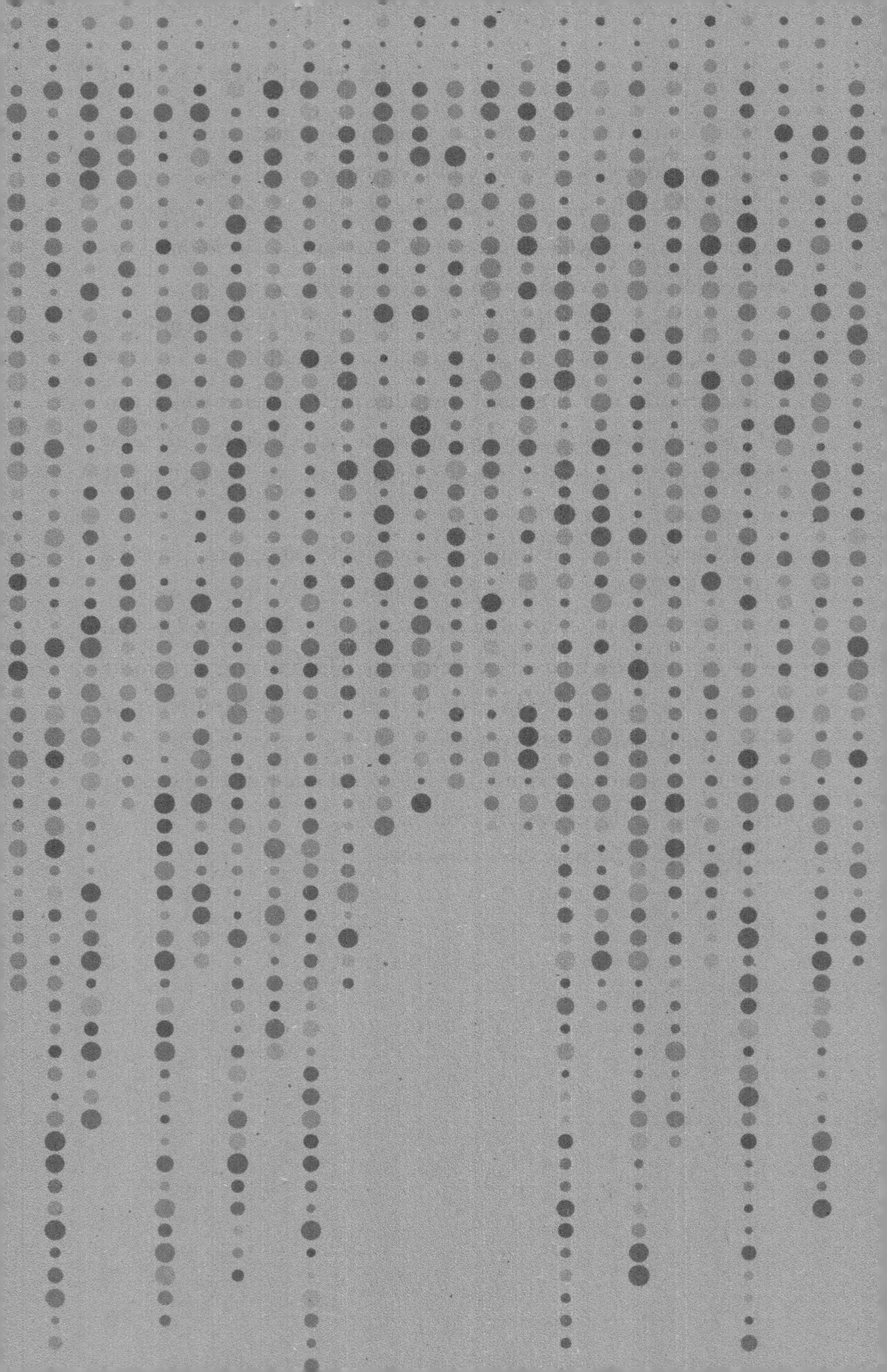

# CHAPTER FOUR

## Fuck If I Know, Part 2

Not that what I have described in the previous chapter isn't a big fuckup already, but the addition of the rules by which platforms operate takes this dysfunction to a whole new level. And when we bring in the known (physical) records and the unknown (digital) records, but now in other parts of an enterprise, the fuck-ups increase.

Two terms that get used interchangeably at times and can be very confusing are MarTech or marketing technology and AdTech or advertising technology.

MarTech is a set of integrated technologies that enables marketing capabilities, such as efficiently and effectively targeting, acquiring, and retaining customers, according to Gartner.[16]

And Gartner defines AdTech as a set of technologies used for managing advertisements across channels, including search, display, video, mobile, and social, with functions for targeting, design, bid management, analytics, optimization, and automation of digital advertising.

16 Gartner, "Definition of Marketing Technology (Martech)" Gartner Information Technology Glossary, accessed October 15, 2023, https://www.gartner.com/en/marketing/glossary/marketing-technology#:~:text=Marketing%20technology%20(martech)%20is%20a,targeting%2C%20acquiring%20and%20retaining%20customers.

These definitions can seem confusing and vague. I think of AdTech as a subset of MarTech. The MarTech world is focused on the known world, where you have information about people coming either from CRM systems or other similar tech, while in the AdTech world, you have anonymous identifiers.

It goes back to our definitions of marketing and advertising. Marketing has goals that go well beyond promoting a brand through paid channels; it involves not only building brand value and growth by acquiring new customers but also sustaining relationships with existing ones. Advertising is an important enabler of marketing, but it's not the only one. Similarly, MarTech has AdTech as a lever, a very important one—but one among many.

The fact that MarTech and AdTech are seen as two different worlds serves as a great illustration of the problem. If you had no idea about any of these existing technologies and were introduced to them, you would have a hard time accepting that AdTech is a subset of MarTech. For all practical purposes, it is not. These platforms are operated by different teams, have minimal connection points, are governed by different budgets in some cases, and your grandmother can probably knit you a full-length woolen coat faster than your ability to stitch together some of the information that comes from these two worlds.

OK, I'm exaggerating slightly—but not by much.

## MarTech–What Is It and Why Does It Exist?

One of the principles I live by is that when someone has done a really good job in assessing a landscape, there is no reason to replicate the effort. Hence, I have borrowed from Terry Kawaja. Terry and LUMA partners are synonymous for their LUMAscapes and the pretty accurate descriptions of various industries. LUMAscapes are landscapes that visualize an entire subset of an industry and categorize the various components of the ecosystem. It acts as a classification chart and captures the total number of companies that operate in the space and the overlaps they have with others across capabilities.

If you take a look at the LUMAscape they produced for marketing technology, the first point you would notice is the potential overlaps that you could have with AdTech. The second point you would probably notice is how technology's influence on the creation of assets makes its presence felt. And the third point you would note is the sheer volume of players involved. It isn't just in AdTech where you see the fragmentation and explosion of services and players. You definitely find that in MarTech as well, which leads to another conclusion: Every single one of these players in many cases presents a decision point: do you use a or b or both?

If you used a provider like Habu to provide a clean room (a mechanism by which datasets get matched without any transfer of PII) to match your first-party data with that of Disney, and then buy media across those resulting audiences in Disney properties, is that MarTech or AdTech? More importantly, it just demonstrates the fluidity between both worlds and the requirements that both have for each other.

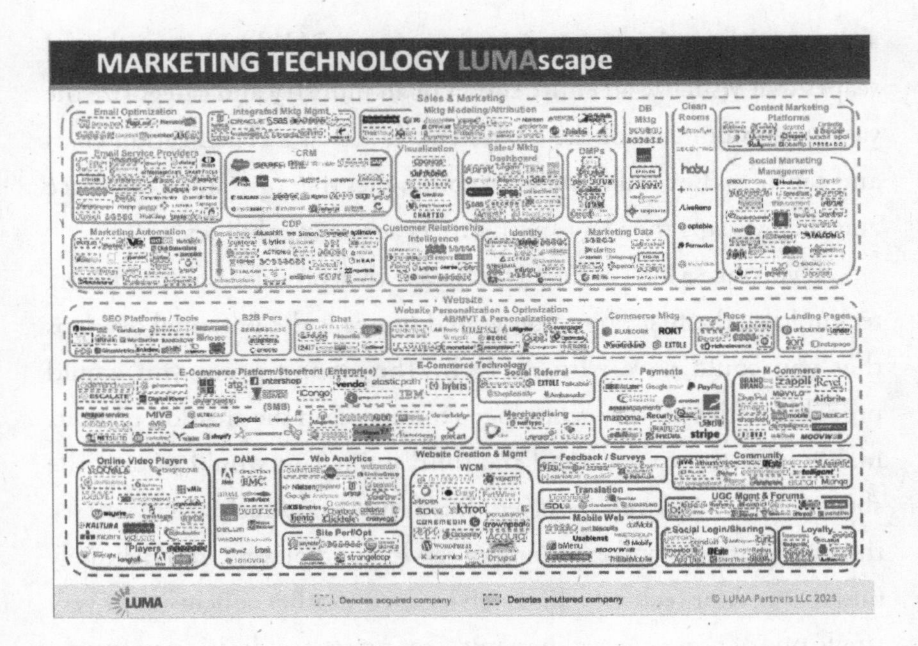


If you have trouble reading these charts, that is an intended effect. Imagine navigating this for your brand. MarTech is all about enabling the marketer to deal with marketing decisions that do not involve paid media like developing websites, driving e-commerce capabilities, online payment systems, and so on. However, as we have demonstrated with the Habu example, the linkages with some of these boxes and those of AdTech are tightly wound.

## The AdTech Maze

A few years ago, it might have been possible to have an AdTech LUMAscape. Today, there just isn't one, and understandably so. There are LUMAscapes for display, convergent TV, mobile, video, out of home, and search to name a few.

In theory, the journey of AdTech began with the simple idea of allowing buyers and sellers to transact audiences on digital assets on the basis of their value to brands. Today, AdTech has become an expense you incur in order to get audiences cheaply.

Publishers are striving to get more direct with marketers; innumerable middle people are plying their trade to get a cut out of the media budget while the platforms sit pretty. The only players who are effectively creating margin in the ecosystem are the platforms; of late, both the buy-side and sell-side platforms are going for each other's jugular with The Trade Desk using Open Path to carve out the supply-side exchanges and the supply-side exchanges looking to connect directly with buyers and disintermediate the demand-side or buy-side platforms.

What a mess….

Of late, when I read about the chaos in the digital market, I am reminded of a quote from late Indian Prime Minister Rajiv Gandhi in the 1980s. There was concern expressed that despite massive amounts of money allocated to poverty alleviation programs, poor people rarely seemed to benefit from them. His response to this concern was to state that for every rupee targeted toward welfare and poverty affiliation, only a fraction, 15 paise (the equivalent of cents), reached the intended beneficiary.[17] Today the Indian government sends cash directly to the accounts of millions of Indians to bypass the many middle people who have historically had a hand in the trough and quite successfully so.

It begs the question: Why haven't marketers and their advertising teams tried the same? The answer is a complicated web of rules, artificial boundaries, and a complete lack of standards that would bedevil the

---

17 Wikipedia, "Only 15 paise reaches the beneficiary," accessed September 20, 2023, https://en.wikipedia.org/wiki/Only_15_paise_reaches_the_beneficiary#:~:text=In%20the%201980s%20Rajiv%20Gandhi,paise%2C%20reached%20the%20intended%20beneficiary.

most disorganized teens. Most of these rules and boundaries have been made up to extract value from the media dollar. Welcome to the jungle.

I thought long and hard about giving an introduction to the platforms and their practices and realized that it wouldn't be an interesting read. I don't want this to be a textbook but the real fun comes in making the connections across some facts that point to a pattern: one that is patently visible but does not get discussed very often. None of what I'm going to write about in the next few paragraphs is going to be new, but what's most interesting is the assumption that many of these practices are legitimate and/or acceptable.

Before we jump into these facts, keep in mind the whole process by which we have created segments and syndicated them to these platforms to find. And also keep in mind that most models of marketing use some variants of "Reach-Is-King." Cross-platform measurement is what's needed most if you have to come up with an accurate estimation of campaign impact.

The following are some facts and attendant principles by which many of the platforms seem to operate:

1) Google, Meta, Amazon, and the other walled gardens don't play well with each other. For example, you are dependent on Meta to let you know what's been achieved in Facebook, Instagram or Threads. You're being asked to trust them.[18] You be the judge.

- The more important implication is that you lose sight of your audience when they move from various parts of the web to Meta. So forget the fancy claims. One cannot control for or measure frequency of exposure between large digital platforms.

---

18 Todd Spangler, "Facebook to Pay $40 Million to Settle Claims It Inflated Video Viewing Data," accessed October 26, 2023, https://variety.com/2019/digital/news/facebook-settlement-video-advertising-lawsuit-40-million-1203361133.

- I call this the *If it doesn't suit me…* principle. It creates silos and perpetuates waste. It's the first step in kneecapping the ability to control frequency of exposure of messages to people.

- Removing cookies has little to do with privacy policies. They have been made into a convenient scapegoat and a demonstration of respect for privacy. And in any case, all privacy policies have done is ask us to accept all cookies—for when you reject them, you get a pretty shitty experience or none at all. Once cookies are gone, it will make it harder to quantify audiences unless a strong identity spine has been matched to first-party data.

- This is the *Blame it on the cookies* principle. Removing cookies in and of itself does not eliminate collection of data; it changes form and shape and access. It also becomes a mechanism to make the rich richer in terms of data while the rest become more reliant on a few.

2) Log files are the nirvana for attribution. They are essentially a register of all digital activity on a platform. Over time, this register has had many of its entries obfuscated and now resembles a tattered piece of cloth that has more holes than fabric. In the good old days, pretty much anyone, whether a DSP, SSP, or an ad server, used to make log files available. Google began removing sensitive information like location and made other information available only through its own data products.

- The other change that accompanied this was aggregation of data. If you gave a query that did not have enough people in a group—for example, how many people follow Crystal Palace (the soccer club) in the Bay Area (this is a nod to Ian Johnson, who is an avid Crystal Palace fan and someone who came up with this analogy)—you wouldn't get a response. Minimums and enough were determined by what you were seeking to group: users, clicks, or conversions.

- Think of the register now having become an account summary, one that was issued only if you had sufficient cash.
- There is a point in the song "American Pie" where the tempo slows, the music is held by only a few strings, and the pathos in Don McLean's voice breaks your heart: *Bye-bye, Miss American Pie...*
- For many of us, it is Bye-bye Attribution. I don't have anything against Google; in fact, I think of all the self-interested players in the ecosystem, they have done more than anyone to navigate the tricky waters of privacy while trying to preserve the fidelity of precision marketing. And they have been the first to engage with others to try and come up with standards, respond to criticism, and change course. Their work on the privacy sandbox deserves praise.
- *Knowledge is great so long as I'm the only one with it.*

3) One of my pet peeves has been the lack of strong connectivity between MarTech and AdTech platforms in areas where it is most needed. If your organization has invested in a DMP or a CDP, then you've probably experienced this. The primary problem arises from the type of identifier used by each platform. Historically, MarTech platforms have worked with PII (e.g., emails), whereas AdTech platforms work with pseudoanonymous identifiers such as cookies. Therefore, you

had customer data being used to send emails or actual mail while advertisers were blind on ad platforms. Of course, the DMPs of yore had third-party cookie synchs available.

- Today, in a perverse twist, due to stringent privacy requirements, you can use identifiers such as email on ad platforms though they have still not gained widespread adoption. Or you could go through the entire process described in the previous chapter to link your first-party data to an external spine and get it onboarded to digital platforms. With no reidentification possible, you entered with individual data about your customers and exited with aggregate data on outcomes.
- In the future, with cookies going away, the ad platforms are far more likely to use identifiers such as emails or aggregate data of some form. However, to be able to syndicate information from your CDP or DMP to an ad platform, you need to have consumer consent around its use and no addition of third-party data along the way according to the likes of Google.
- The future is going to depend on an organization's ability to collect and use first-party data where consent is obtained and recorded. That's a hell of an ask for most marketers, and even in categories where there is a natural business need to collect information, such as the financial sector, the volume of data collected will, in most cases, not be sufficient to improve effectiveness the way it was hyped before. And this would beg the question: Is the juice worth the squeeze? What is the investment required to sustain a first-party ecosystem in order to connect with the likes of Google and model your audiences or create new ones? And will they result in the ROI needed to justify the expense?

- *Not all connections are equal.* There is an assumption baked into many platform sales pitches that syndication and connectivity are seamless; they are not. And in many cases, they are not as automated as they seem.

4) If you've noticed, I haven't mentioned a lot about Meta or Apple. That's because Meta won't connect to other players and hence will remain an island. While some of the processes to match audiences, etc., would look the same with Meta, since it doesn't connect to anyone else, it will mean a duplication of effort.

- Apple will always try to disrupt the advertising model because (a) it can and (b) it does have the opportunity to redefine data-driven marketing (I'm not quite sure that it wants to though). As I discuss in chapters 6 and 7 on how we can make data-driven marketing work, Apple's approach around privacy provides a plank that could make marketers and consumers happy.

- *Islands have more value than oceans do.* There is a perverse incentive in managing *dis*-connectivity between platforms that reduces fidelity of decision-making.

The situation does not improve when you look at the Open Web or the dark oceans as I call them.

Bob Liodice, CEO of the ANA, has been quite focused on unmasking value generation in the programmatic media buying industry for a decade with ANA reports coming out in regular intervals. When I spoke to him in June 2023, a week before the Cannes Lions festival, the ANA was about to issue a report on Programmatic Media Supply Chain Transparency, a study focused on the Open Web as opposed to the walled gardens such as Google, et al. The report makes for disturbing reading:

> *Twenty-one member companies participated, with the data collection period between September 2022 and January 2023. That consisted of $123 million in ad spend and 35.5 billion impressions, mostly classic banner and video ads. Qualitative work supplemented quantitative research.*
>
> *Key findings:*
>
> *1. Information asymmetry is a serious issue for advertisers.*
>
> *2. Data access is lacking, leading to inefficiencies and waste.*
>
> *3. There are misaligned incentives as advertisers prioritize cost over value.*
>
> *4. The average campaign ran on 44,000 websites, leading to more waste.*
>
> *5. Made-for-Advertising websites represent 21 percent of impressions.*
>
> *6. Sustainability efforts can be enhanced with productive programmatic media buying.*
>
> *7. The previously identified "unknown delta" can be virtually eliminated with a full path log-level data (LLD) analysis.*[19]

19 ANA, "ANA Programmatic Media Supply Chain Transparency Study—First Look," accessed September 12, 2023, https://www.ana.net/miccontent/show/id/rr-2023-06-ana-programmatic-transparency-first-look.

As Bob put it to me, "Do we need forty-four thousand websites in a campaign? No. We know that if you limit that purchase to a couple hundred websites, you can reach 95 percent of your targeted audience. Incentives are misaligned, leading to very poor media investment decisions, which does relatively little to boost the prospect of your brands. So, while programmatic media is a phenomenal tool, it's a phenomenal tool when it's well executed, when you have the data to make the decisions. And by the way, I'm only speaking about the Open Web. I'm not speaking about the walled gardens, because that's a whole different level of data transparency, which is a huge issue."

I'm often told by industry insiders, and you might be thinking the same: Would we behave differently if we were in the same position as Google or the others? There is also a sentiment expressed that platforms have the right to set their own business rules, and who are we to question them? After all, they have provided billions of people access to products and services at no cost in most cases.

I'm also acutely aware that I might not be invited to work at some of these companies in the future and that you should definitely doubt my career growth advice. While I do have some sympathy for these arguments, I ask: Are they universally applicable? In other words, would we accept these arguments if they were made in other product categories by other companies?

Take your mobile phone. Try dialing any of your contacts or any number anywhere on the planet. As long as you're paying for the capability to make calls, you can connect to any of them. How many times do you wonder about the carrier, the make and model, or the plan that the person you're calling is on or uses? Do you have to bother with a map that gives you mechanisms on how to convert your voice for Samsung phones if you're using one made by Apple?

If the telecom industry operated by the principles by which digital platforms operate, you would be doing just that. And probably every alternate word you said would be lost in the ether leading to some interesting conversations.

There is a vital distinction between the two industries that makes this even more stark. In the case of telecom, the consumer does not have any role in creating the product. The ability to connect does not exist because of people; telcos have to ensure that the infrastructure works independent of people using them. In the ad platform business, data, which is the product that is effectively allowing for transactions, gets created only when the consumer participates in the ecosystem. The monetization abilities of some of these platforms will decline sharply with little to no consumer participation in creating data.

The only argument I can think of in support of creating silos is the cost of providing free content and services. However, even this is under threat as many streaming platforms and other content providers seek to benefit from both subscriber revenue and ad revenue.

So why the heck do we not have any standards? Enforceable standards are the reason why our phones operate the way they do. Bandwidth is auctioned, standards such as 5G, etc., are agreed upon, and we don't end up with cross-connections. Telcos are free to add services or price their products as they see fit but they don't artificially create silos in an attempt to benefit themselves.

And no, I'm not a Luddite intent on believing that all is wrong with us and there isn't any great work being done. There is great work that gets produced, but it is overwhelmed by mediocrity posing as excellence in a marketplace disfigured by rules that cost both consumers and brands a lot of wasted time, energy, and money. I'm not even getting to the impact on the climate just yet because I worry that might get me canceled in today's political environment.

If the marketing ecosystem especially as it pertains to advertising was likened to a globe, it would be dominated by dark oceans, a few brightly lit islands, and a number of mirages.

Why the heck is our industry (by which I mean all of marketing) so discombobulated? Fuck if I know.

But do regulators know better?

## The Regulators

Reading about laws, policies, and regulations puts me to sleep. It has since I was trying to muscle through understanding various conventions, constitutions, and societal policies in high school, and I vowed to myself that I wouldn't ever put others through this. But there are always broken promises, and I have no choice but to make you wade through this web of rules that seem to be built for one purpose and end up delivering another. It's necessary in order to establish the connection between the actual issues faced by people and the marketing industry in general and the response of the regulators, which (spoiler alert!) hasn't been aligned or great.

My only promise is to keep this section as brief as possible with an attempt to cut to the chase and not drift.

To its credit, the EU was the first to institute data regulations and create laws around privacy protection, and it has maintained its lead in defining rights of individuals around how their data is used.

According to the United Nations Conference on Trade and Development (UNCTAD), 71 percent of countries have some form of data protection and privacy legislation; 9 percent have draft legislation, 15 percent have none, and 5 percent have no data.[20]

---

20 UNCTAD, "Data Protection and Privacy Legislation Worldwide," accessed September 28, 2023, https://unctad.org/page/data-protection-and-privacy-legislation-worldwide.

You can actually download a file that shows the total number of legislations, with links to each one of those—and it currently runs to 241 rows. The most important ones are those passed by Europe, different US states, and China. For the purposes of this book, I've only considered legislation passed in the EU, the United Kingdom, and the United States.

There are some key principles that are common across all of them, and many of them are modeled on the GDPR of the EU. The other legislation that has serious impact is the CCPA passed and amended by California. Given California's outsize contribution to the US and global economies, this legislation has a fair amount of impact.

## GDPR–Gross Denial of Promotion Rights

The GDPR is quite comprehensive and covers any information that can be tied to an individual. It basically wipes out distinctions between cookies, mobile identifiers, names, email addresses, etc. If the information points to an individual, then it's in scope. It creates clear rules for processors and controllers of data. And it outlines six different legal bases for processing the personal information of anyone in the EU: (1) consent from an individual allowing one to collect and process information about that person while making sure that the individual is aware of the purpose of that collection; (2) contractual purposes; for example, a merchant is going to need the purchaser's credit card information to process the payment for something they are willing to buy; (3) compliance with legal obligations of the controller (entity or person using data); (4) protect vital interests of the individual; (5) national security or public interest; and (6) legitimate interest.[21]

The last one is ambiguous and contentious. Legitimate interest pertains to situations where the interests of those who control the data outweigh the interests of the data subjects or those whose data is being collected. The law itself is vague in use cases, but businesses have made the case that their right to exist depends on data collection and therefore outweighs other interests. This has effectively been shot down and has not been held up by the European Union. In other words, a business cannot use legitimate interest to justify processing data for marketing purposes.

These principles seem quite clear, and the rights enshrined seem so as well: the right to delete data, the right to access, the right to opt out, the right to transfer data, the right to be informed, and the right to not be discriminated against.

But there is no legal basis to collect information for the purpose of advertising or marketing. According to a dated study from 2015, prior to GDPR being enacted in 2018 (Economic Contribution of Digital Advertising in Europe by IHS Markit), digital advertising contributed 25 billion euros directly and another 118 billion euros indirectly. If we added other effects such as sales induced by advertising, etc., the contribution adds up to 526 billion euros.

You can quibble with the numbers all you want—and many will—but the impact is significant. Add the estimated six million jobs that were supported by digital advertising, the impact becomes clear. Yet there was no consideration for such a sizable industry in one of the most prolific data protection laws on the planet.

21 Data Guidance, "Comparing Privacy Laws: GDPR v. CCPA," accessed September 22, 2023, chrome-extension://efaidnbmnnnibpcajpcglclefindmkaj/https://fpf.org/wp-content/uploads/2018/11/GDPR_CCPA_Comparison-Guide.pdf.

## CCPA–California Changes Privacy for America

The CCPA had a different path to becoming legislation. It originated as a ballot initiative, garnered sufficient momentum such that the California legislature agreed to pass a less restrictive law in return for the withdrawal of the ballot initiative. It became law in 2020.

I always find it interesting to read about the history of the CCPA. One of the many individuals involved in piloting and providing momentum to this legislation is Alastair Mactaggart. He is the founder of Californians for Privacy, the group that collected enough signatures to get a privacy policy in place. He is also a real estate developer (president of the Emerald Fund); he has built condos, apartments, shopping centers, et al., in San Francisco.

What's funny is how the real estate industry works with data.

Any real estate transaction is a matter of public record and can be accessed by anyone, including in the Great State of California despite two big legislations covering privacy. In other words, I don't need consent to find out where you live and how much you paid to whom for your condo, and I can basically use it as a proxy for determining your economic status, but I need your permission to drop a cookie to see if you saw my ad for a chocolate bar.

I've always wanted to write the above paragraph; in fact, if you told me that the only satisfaction I am going to get out of writing this book is that paragraph and that this book will never be bought by a soul, I would remain gratified. It was so cathartic to write that paragraph about an inconsistency that doesn't seem to have been noticed by most. Anyway, rant over.

While there are a number of similarities with GDPR in terms of protections, there are some key differences as well with the CCPA.

There is no clear legal basis for collecting data outlined, and financial and health information are omitted, primarily because there are other laws that account for them. The CCPA is focused more on consumer consent than on other means.

This gets reflected in the right to opt out. The CCPA gives people the right to opt out of their personal information being sold for business purposes while other uses of the data can be retained. If a person opts out, there is no legitimate basis available for a business to argue that the information can still be used. Under GDPR, people need to opt in to allow their data to be collected and used.

Not to stop there, the Californians then enacted the California Privacy Rights Act of 2020 or CPRA (Californians Propose more Rules for America), which had more protections, expanded provisions, tripled the amount of fines as before, and created an agency to help implement this.

According to an initial estimate widely reported by the media, companies would spend about $55 billion for compliance.[22] I'm pretty sure they weren't planning on eating that cost; I'm sure a small part of the inflation in prices is down to these laws.

Other states have now decided to follow this path.

## The Rest of the United States—We Can Do It Too!

Apart from California, the states of Colorado, Connecticut, Indiana, Iowa, Montana, Oregon, Tennessee, Texas, Virginia, and Utah have all

22 Lauren Feiner, "California's New Privacy Law Could Cost Companies a Total of $55 Billion to Get in Compliance," https://www.cnbc.com/2019/10/05/california-consumer-privacy-act-ccpa-could-cost-companies-55-billion.html, accessed October 1, 2023.

passed their own version of comprehensive data privacy legislation.[23] Most of these legislations are similar, with options for state residents to opt out of targeted advertising and sale of their personal data, with opt-outs being the favored mechanism.

And you can bet more are down the pike. The one that you will find missing is a US federal law. You're unlikely to see it anytime soon; while both parties agree that we probably need some law, some question whether there is a crying need for one. Unless you've been in a business that's forced to reckon with multiple similar laws with slight differences that are guaranteed to drive you crazy, there is no crying need. Unless you want to make sure you don't lose the battle on AI with China, there is no crying need.

## Why Am I So Upset?

It's a legitimate question, I think. After all the criticism of the previous chapters where I've outlined the many ways by which data-driven advertising and marketing have failed people, it would be fair to expect me to support the regulators. Except I think they have worsened the problem.

I remember when I learned how to drive in Delhi. If you're worried about my driving capabilities, I tested and passed the license test in the United Kingdom. I've been assured that the UK's is one of the hardest driving tests to pass. So you're safe to sit in my car. But back when I was learning to drive in Delhi, I had an instructor who decided to issue turn commands at the very last second. I would approach intersections with trepidation because I had no idea whether I would be expected to turn or continue straight.

---

23 Andrew Folks, "US State Privacy Legislation Tracker," updated October 20, 2023, accessed October 26, 2023, https://iapp.org/resources/article/us-state-privacy-legislation-tracker/.

On one such occasion, as I was in the middle of an intersection, my instructor casually asked me to turn left. Since I was close to passing the midpoint of the intersection, I braked hard and turned. Except I pressed the accelerator instead of the brake and the car went flying around the corner. Motorists, pedestrians, my instructor, a street dog, and I were all equally shocked. Good intentions and all that… yet poor execution. I'm sure many of us have pressed the accelerator while in reverse gear, assuming we were in drive.

Regulators, Mr. Taggart, and European and American legislators are guilty of the same. Great intentions combined with poor execution has led to the exact opposite of what was intended to be achieved.

Here are some signature achievements of these laws:

1) By making consent from consumers a critical basis for collecting and using information, these laws have empowered platforms and businesses that have a strong incentive to attract people over those that are either starting up or are niche content providers or have not invested in infrastructure to collect the data in the first place. In other words, the likes of Google and Meta have benefited while the open internet is under threat. Even if consumers do not give permission to Google or Meta to sell their information, in the United States, they can still aggregate groups of people, attach broad attributes to them, and use that for monetization.

2) Compliance costs have gone up with the result that entire armies of lawyers, privacy experts, and privacy tech have become another overhead for marketing.

3) The laws do not create a common set of standards that everyone needs to follow. These are laws of overt protection without a set of standards that support execution. For example,

anywhere in the world today, if you want to build an airplane, there is a set of technical standards that needs to be adhered to. Where are the technical standards for privacy? Cookies, per se, are not violative of legislation, yet tech platforms determine these standards with the result that you can get a certain standard of privacy if you can afford a thousand-dollar phone and another standard if you can't. Philosophies and business models determine the extent of privacy citizens can hope to get. And the poor marketer, whose name has been dragged through the mud as an encouraging participant in violating people's privacy, is none the wiser.

4) Ironically, all these laws have just increased waste. If you cannot do cross-site tracking—in other words, follow behavior across sites that don't belong to the same entity (go from Forbes.com to Apple.com as an example)—the marketer does not know whether the person on Apple.com is the same person who saw the ad on Forbes.com. Platforms claim that user privacy is protected, but the user ends up seeing the same ads a number of times (more than necessary) and the marketer wastes their money in showing the same message to the same people. Who gains? The technology platform. It wouldn't matter if they had bought the product; in many cases, there would be no way of knowing. More the ads, more the spend, more the waste, and more the carbon emissions. Have people been accurately informed about the choices they have?

5) Ostensibly many of these laws were inspired by the Cambridge Analytica scandal with Facebook; however, political advertising has not been restricted. In the United States, it is still possible to use the likes of Meta or Google to target segments

> of people based on various interests and attitudes. And because in the United States personal information can be used even if people have opted out of their data being sold, analytics can still draw inferences that are useful. So, have these laws really changed much?

People, whom these laws are designed to protect, have seen their ad experiences continue to worsen; marketers continue to spend frightful amounts of money chasing personalization at scale and an entire privacy industry has reaped benefits.

Pretty much the only segment that has gained are the platforms themselves. It's strange but not illogical to see news items that announce tech executives getting grilled over data privacy laws, etc., while also reporting on ad business rebounds for these platforms.

That's why I have angst; an entire set of people having their reputations questioned and tarnished while others have made merry without fundamentally changing much for either the consumer or the marketer.

There will be one group of regulators that does get some basics. I spoke to David Cohen, CEO of the Internet Advertising Bureau (IAB), an industry body that seeks to drive standards and represent the interests of the internet advertising ecosystem. As David explains, the FTC or Federal Trade Commission does give some common sense-based advice: Make consent policies easy to understand for people and don't hold on to data forever; delete it when not needed. Those are two steps that the industry should be taking right now.

## But I Thought Advertising Was About Creative???

At last, messaging gets a mention. It is weird that I've written a lot about data and precision and not talked at all about creativity, which is what most people expect from the word *advertising*. It is, in truth, a reflection of reality: creativity has become divorced from the marketing and advertising processes. Ever since media agencies and other specializations have split from the creative function, the divorce has sped on, fueled by data and technology.

On one of my many required trips to the Cannes Lions festival back in 2017, an annual event celebrating the best of advertising and where the who's who of the marketing and advertising world come together for a week, I was invited by a creative agency to address their leadership team. I was on a high, having been a part of the jury for the Data Lions and having spent a fair amount of time judging really great work. I still believe that the best use of Cannes is spent discussing work and getting familiar with great ideas, which most people rarely do, and it's a real shame.

My talk to the agency centered around *Moneyball,* the movie based on the book *Moneyball: The Art of Winning an Unfair Game* by Michael Lewis. My thesis was that the advertising and marketing industries were being disrupted by data the very same way baseball was disrupted by sabermetrics a decade or more ago. I proceeded to proselytize the value of data and how it could add to advertising. Of course, being a true data nerd, I didn't have much in terms of how this impacted messaging.

There was a fair sense of doom and gloom at the end of my presentation. I had set out to inspire people and had ended up achieving the opposite effect. Maybe it was my belief in the inevitability of change or the belief that this change was great for everyone and not accepting it was not an option; either way, the impact was heavy. One of the audience members asked me a pointed question.

"When I was a young girl, I used to watch ads for products not meant for me. But I remember them, and today some of my brand loyalty is informed by those memories. If we end up becoming precise, does a brand then not miss out on these favorable outcomes?"

In that moment, the question seemed naïve and one driven by sentiment rather than logic. Coming from the world of media, where scale is the altar at which we worship, such individual instances are often not given the importance they should. I don't quite remember my response, but I'm pretty sure it was vague and not very helpful. Because I didn't have an answer to the question.

When I was studying for my postgraduate diploma in marketing communications from Mudra Institute of Communications Ahmedabad (MICA), I used to, like others, spend hours in the library watching ads. I would read through Desmond Morris's *Manwatching* and try and watch for all kinds of cues in the films. One of my favorite ads was the Mystery Squeaking Noise ad by Volkswagen.[24] It never fails to amaze me to this day.

When my wife and I were considering our first car in the UK, fifteen years later, Volkswagen was right there at the top of the list. And though we did not buy it, I'd say it entered the list without much consideration: I just could not have a car shopping list and not have a Volkswagen in it.

Over the years, we in the data and technology community have consistently preached the idea of personalization at scale. And personalization has had a lens of individuality to it. The message or the

---

24 https://www.youtube.com/watch?v=JF-KJ5-KNQk. If you haven't seen it, I highly recommend you watch it.

creative was an afterthought. The underlying assumption was that account planners, strategists, and creative directors were creating broad brush stories that very rarely resonated with people and that the way people consumed media would be the way they consumed stories about brands. Some of it might have been true, but in our desire to correct it, we have made the problem worse.

Research shows that people get annoyed most by ads repeating themselves or getting followed by product ads despite their having bought it online or having rejected it earlier. I talk about this later in the ensuing pages.

Terry Kawaja of LUMA Partners is always a hoot to listen to but hidden beneath all the parodies and wit is a really sharp mind and a unique ability to write upside down on a glass table. When I met Terry in his offices in New York, we discussed a wide range of topics including his views on creativity and the lack of connection between efficiency and efficacy.

Two areas he spoke about were the impending impact of AI and how, as is the norm, the industry was focused on job dislocation and the lack of connection between media and creative data. We have built armies of people to monetize media while the lack of connection with creative leads to a sharp drop in effectiveness. AI can solve for this but only if it is deployed the right way and the focus is on creating amazing creative that connects with what the data is saying about people.

## A Summary of All the Fuck-Ups

We have gone through a lot of fuck-ups, but if you boil it down, the story is quite simple. Here it is.

Advertising has always been about stories around products, services, and solutions wrapped in emotional or rational messages. We thought we never had the ability to make it seem like every message was meant for everyone. Our assumption was that powerful stories alone wouldn't do it.

So, we decided to use digital media and data to personalize at scale. Along this journey, we promised anyone who needed promises that we would be able to address individuals and measure success and answer fundamental questions that many major parts of marketing could not aspire to do.

As we diverted spend toward digital platforms that initially promised addressability and accountability, we allowed those very platforms to balkanize the internet for their own benefit, all the while looking the other way. Soon, metrics fragmented, and it became harder to tell what was working and what was not.

Privacy activists and regulators latched on to big tech and its claims and ended up enacting big privacy bills with laudable objectives but no underlying standards to execute them. And by the way, almost all these bills have empowered the very platforms they purport to dislike or take down.

Surprisingly people, the constituency in whose name this entire mess is conducted, seem to have different priorities. They don't like watching ads because they are repetitive or annoying and frustrating. There also does not seem to be much of an appetite for experiences that seem creepy like tracking across devices, usage of location data, and so on.[25] They are also unaware of both the costs imposed by regulations that are probably impacting their financials in different ways and their own employment prospects in a digital economy that doesn't have reasonable standards.

Marketing leaders who really just want to inspire people to embrace their brands and develop relationships of value with

---

25 Schomer, accessed October 20, 2023.

customers instead find themselves grasping at cost control as a laudable objective. Pushed by CFOs asking simple questions around ROI and CEOs struggling to explain expenses to investors pushing for margin expansion, CHEAP, COST-EFFICIENCY, DROP MY CPM (cost per thousand…), MITIGATE INFLATION, TOO EXPENSIVE, NONWORKING MEDIA and others became the words uttered in many meetings all with the same result: a race to the bottom.

And what about the platforms? They want growth in users and services and ad dollars in many cases to fund their expansion. I bet they don't want to find themselves constantly living with positive earnings reports and threats to be fined or disbanded chasing them at the same time.

On balance, weirdly, both the big tech platforms and privacy activists can claim success or at least some measure of comfort. Neither marketers nor people can claim much.

We can put men on the moon, make space stations, get rockets to land back on launch pads, 3D print missiles, teach machines to think for themselves, find a vaccine for a global pandemic in under three years, create national identity spines like the UIDAI (Unique Identification Authority of India) with 1.35 billion identities, but cannot tell how many times someone watched an ad for a product across media and platforms.

Why does it matter? Because more than a trillion dollars a year is being spent on marketing, with a fair amount of waste because of these reasons. Even assuming waste is at a modest 20 percent, that is $200 billion. The number is likely to be closer to half a trillion; no one can say for sure, and this number does not consider knock-on effects. Companies may want to reinvest that money elsewhere in their people, new products, new markets, maybe take on more lucrative challenges that haven't been adopted because of budget issues.

In the grand scheme of things, it might seem small.

It's a $200 billion-plus fuckup.

# CHAPTER FIVE

## The Saga Continues

*Ross* sat back and watched his eight-year-old daughter kick the soccer ball to her older brother and scream as he missed blocking it. "Daddy told me I could be better than you!" Ross heard his daughter's voice come through the French windows, making it seem like she had a tinny voice. He smiled as he looked at the two screens on the desk in front of him again. The deck was ready, his story arc was fixed and had been rehearsed with his team multiple times this week, and instead of having to burn the midnight oil, his material was comfortably ready, polished, and good to go. Except…the results weren't transformational.

They were nowhere close to the results he had promised his boss last year during the annual strategy retreat of the airline. The board had been there as well, and he had been invited to present his strategy to them; for the first time in eight years he had received an audience with the board. And he wasn't disappointed. The board had been supportive and had encouraged him to report back the next year on results of his strategies. As CMO of the airline, Ross had consolidated more power under his belt by expanding his team and remit and had changed the agency driving brand transformation. His budgets had gone up, as had his team size.

It was time to head back to Palm Beach again for the annual retreat. But this time the board would be expecting to see results, as would his boss, CEO Richard Linkwater, who had been under a minor cloud for the past six months over various public gaffes and had come to be seen as a liability by some. This could be Ross's moment… or not.

The numbers weren't impressive. Sales were up, holiday package sales were up, but they were in line with spend increases. There was no disproportionate boom that he had anticipated. He didn't feel any the wiser either on why all efforts had led to this situation. Sarah had done all she could to create a story based on analytics, and he might have even got over some of the obvious gaps in data if the environment hadn't been so charged. If nothing, he expected his boss to be sharp and bring a very traditional approach to issues while softly undermining Ross on the important areas of performance and growth.

The airline had missed its passenger growth numbers. Yet again. Despite all the newfangled tactics his team had deployed backed by investments in a tech stack, they were still losing share. The only people happy in tomorrow's meeting would be the procurement teams. Their cost goals had all been reached. Prices paid for agencies, media, technology vendors, creators, and content sponsorships had all shown drops. This was another concern for Ross, ironically; if costs hadn't been so aggressively cut, some of his metrics would be looking a lot worse.

So, what in the world had not gone per plan?

For starters, #AirlineGate didn't help. A passenger had been brutally shoved by a stewardess for insisting on an extra drink and hurling the choicest racist epithets at her. Turned out the whole incident had been a setup. The passenger had asked her friends to capture the event on video and it went up instantly on TikTok and became another episode of the culture wars. The stewardess was Black, the passenger White, and the airline was stuck in a world of gray. A decision was taken to compensate the passenger while putting the stewardess on notice, and lo and behold everything that was ever said about race relations in America was said again. *The New Yorker* put the airline on the cover and showed two people marked Black and White struggling to get through the aisle. The plane was America, but it didn't help the airline one bit.

Apart from the usual bigots, normally decent people joined in the fight, helped by the anonymity of whatever choice of poisonous environment they preferred.

The airline struggled to combat the swirl of news; over the years public relations was seen as a cost, and the department had been steadily reduced. Apart from getting interviews for the big boss and a healthy lobbying budget, there wasn't much there. So, it fell on marketing to change the narrative.

Every single partner of the airline scrambled to help, but it wasn't enough. Multiple ads touting customer service or cheap fares aired across media immediately after the blip (as the airline's marketing team began calling it), bringing #AirlineGate to the top of the trending Tweets (or Xs?) list. What was a service issue swiftly became a marketing issue; the board started asking Ross for his responses to the various items written in the press. PR was a part of marketing, but structurally, it had reported directly to the CEO, whereas once it had been under the chief human resources officer under the guise of handling internal employee communications. This wasn't widely known with the result that Ross ended up fielding queries and becoming the face of the response.

No one could say with certainty that this crisis had impacted passenger growth numbers. There were no mass cancellations; no sudden increases or decreases. Brand favorability took a hit for sure, but the expected drop in ticket sales did not come about. For years, models had been built internally by marketing to measure the impact of brand favorability to sales. Now those connections looked shaky at best.

None of the airline's competitors had a presence rivaling his. The economy had grown as expected, leisure travel was booming, and corporate America was beginning to travel again. Yet the airline was not able to grow as expected in either the low-fare leisure segment or the business segment. It didn't follow any of the previous scripts of social media backlash. But Ross was sure it was there.

*Why* was the question he was going to get asked tomorrow, and he had fifteen hours to come up with a cogent response. The prospect of discussing this with his boss and the main players at the airline didn't make him feel any pleasure. If he managed to navigate through tomorrow's meeting, he would get a chance to again hobnob with some of the most important executives powering one of the biggest airlines in America in the Sunshine State.

*Sarah* sat still, straining to focus on the charts lying in front of her, rubbing her eyes from the glare of the small but sharp table light. She preferred printouts; she was old school that way. Physical copies always allowed her to grasp figures better, she could circle around, jump between sheets, and find the link between them. That was hard to do this year. She couldn't find anything beyond the obvious. In fact, if she were honest, the campaign would have to go down as being unsuccessful. Even if she discounted the impact of social backlash, there were signs that the budget increases were not producing the impact they were expected to. She had no idea how she was going to help Ross, her boss, defend the execution of the past six months.

Her mind went back to the review meeting three days ago with Ari, the agency head on the business, Stuart, the e-com head, and Ross. Once again, she was the only woman in the room and was sick of the infighting and posturing that didn't make anything clearer. She had tried to steer the meeting in the direction of getting specific answers but was soon caught up in a maelstrom of implementation minutiae, regression methods, and log file obfuscation. She could sense that Ross had been equally fed up. Most movies or shows depict corporate meetings as swift affairs where people speak their minds and decisions are made ultrafast. That was complete horseshit.

Meetings ground you down, proceeded at a glacial pace, and often totally sidestepped the issues they were meant to address. Ross never confronted Ari and Stuart on working together and being transparent on attribution approaches or deals struck with third parties; Stuart was never transparent about what he was really doing with his e-commerce budget, and Ari had learned fast that he needed to hold his cards close to his chest.

It boiled down to this. There was clear data about the impact of optimization within the airline's assets. Stuart could talk about the sales achieved through addressable media and affiliate channels. He could also point out efficiencies achieved by his team in driving costs down. On the other hand, Ari spoke in terms of big brand placements, media ideas that were feted by the industry press and the absolute number of ad exposures that his team had generated. He too pointed out cost-efficiency gains and had a projected reach number that was an estimation at best. There was no clear verification that the audience segments had worked well. There was little to no commonality between the audience segments leveraged by Stuart and Ari. And since Ari wasn't allowed to collect information from the airline's website, he was operating in ether.

This was a common problem across the industry. Ari represented the brand budget and Stuart the performance budget. People who were ultimately the recipients of both didn't make any such distinctions, yet the industry did, putting money in neat buckets. Sarah was always amazed that such buckets existed because any half-decent MMM would show you that brand metrics did impact sales. Richard Linkwater was on record saying that brand choices were made in a retail or e-commerce environment. That just wasn't true.

In any case, she couldn't answer some basic questions: Did the brand advertising positively impact online sales and if so by how much? Did the social backlash impact sales and if so by how much? What was the true impact of Stuart's optimization? In other words, if the brand campaign had not run, would his tactical optimizations have been as successful? And anyway, what did success look like? If costs were kept out, the campaign hadn't achieved its impact goals. If she used baseline models from the past, she estimated that they could have spent 20 percent less and achieved the same outcome.

Normally she would have constructed another model and demonstrated the impact of different efforts on sales. But with the total outcome not being great, she struggled to reconcile opposing viewpoints and claimed contributions. The social backlash had created a haze; there was no past precedent, no industry benchmark on impact except in a very broad sense. She had prepared the model and shown it to Ross, who was inscrutable. Whether he was going to use her slides and talk through what channels worked and what didn't was anyone's guess, but she couldn't see any other way out of it.

Sarah sighed, as she started massaging her temples with her forefingers. Tomorrow was going to be a long day as her boss presented to Richard. She would be in the room for backup; she hoped that no one would notice her and that the conversation would be collegial. Who was she kidding?

*Ari* was finishing dinner and catching a late Yankees game on the big screen TV in his living room. The Yankees were destined to probably finish last this season in the division, but Ari was always hopeful; maybe this was the year that the Yankees would finally accelerate when it was needed. Being a New York sports fan had given him tons of patience dealing with professional disappointment. As expected, the airline account hadn't gone the way he wanted it to, and as expected Rebecca Stone, the agency's managing director and his boss, was hot on his ass, ready to fire him before the airline fired them. Neither he nor Rebecca would be in the room tomorrow for the review presentation to the airline's CEO. That was a relief because he worried that if she was present, she would be quick to do a *mea culpa* and pin it on him, even if not needed, just to see the back of Ari.

It was such a shit show. Every single commitment made by him and his team to the airline prior to the pitch had fallen by the wayside as it just became impossible to wrangle different people to align on approaches or processes or just share data. He found it ridiculous that he couldn't optimize linear TV on sales data; by the time it came back, it was too late, aggregated, and sometimes inaccurate. To top it off, he had developed a positive dislike of Stuart and his cronies. He had very little respect or patience for them. Though he knew that somewhere they were all trying to go for the same goal, it felt more competitive and adversarial than ever before.

He had to prepare for battle before every meeting with Stuart; his only defense was declining cost. His team had negotiated costs down but had also smartly negotiated for extra value that was really helpful during the PR crisis. Even requests to get access to the right journalists had been passed down to him and he had done his best leveraging his sales relationships to set up interviews with big reporters for the airline.

He couldn't make conclusive claims though, and what hurt him the most was that Stuart could. Even if brand advertising had led to demand creation, Stuart was the only one who could actually claim that he had converted a piece of interest into a sale. Ari's favorite was the pizza redemption coupon analogy. You could take a free pizza coupon and distribute it to everyone who was standing in a line to buy pizzas. All of them would take you up on it, and your redemption rate would be 100 percent. But that didn't mean that the coupon drove the behavior or the sale; it was the other way around. He suspected that a number of Stuart's claims were just that—benefits of all the mass media messaging that he, Ari, had deployed.

The fight had drained him and his team. The enthusiasm of the airline being the biggest and newest account had long since worn off. Now people in his team were trying to get off the account; they couldn't deal with the pressure and the lack of achievement anymore. His review with Rebecca was coming up—that wasn't a conversation he was looking forward to. The next few days were not going to be easy.

The only ally he had was Sarah, but she was stuck trying to answer questions for which he could honestly not provide answers. His professional integrity drove him to push for greater heights but in this case, he was still at base camp. He was just waiting for the axe to fall.

*Stuart* was still on his email, typing away in staccato bursts despite the obvious irritation of his wife. She was trying to catch up on *House of the Dragon*; Stuart couldn't care less about dragons and politics; he saw enough political games in his job that he didn't want to relive them at night. To be fair to his wife, it was 10:30 at night, an ideal time to watch debauchery on screen.

Stuart was trying to convince Sarah to drop a few slides from her boss's deck. He was worried that interpretations could be made of certain data that could involve questioning his outlay for the rest of the year. He found it weird that the head of analytics reported exclusively to the CMO and had no reporting line to him. He had a good professional relationship with Sarah, but at the end of the day Ross alone conducted her performance review.

The issue at stake was the correct mix between brand and performance budgets. He didn't love the differentiation, but it did allow him to focus and, more importantly, drive a greater outlay for his team. He had been successful in torpedoing the agency's audience efforts. He didn't believe in arbitrary definitions; for a budget airline, despite all its intentions of going premium, most people could be customers. Reach was all that counted. He thought of himself as the hunter. The best place to hunt in a forest is at the watering hole. The obvious difference between drinking water and flying escaped him. Stuart could be quite blind that way when he got focused on his goal. He could convince himself and others in his orbit about his intentions.

Sarah had managed to build a full funnel model: one that broke through silos between brand and performance budgets. Her model attempted to explain the relationship between various inputs in media with business outcomes and other brand parameters like favorability and intention to purchase. Some conclusions were obvious, and he didn't have an issue with them. He agreed that the media buys and sponsorships focused on corporations had triggered greater awareness and favorability for the brand, resulting in more business-class seats getting bought by non-leisure customers.

One of the main conclusions, though, troubled him. The model showed that as brand dollars dried up, the website and app traffic declined rapidly, and sales numbers dropped. The acquisition budget spent by Stuart and his team did not seem to be as successful in pulling new customers in without the support of the brand. Stuart's contention was that the audiences attracted by the brand campaign were fickle and not core customers of the airline in the first place. And that making the airline a choice for such people in the absence of a brand campaign would take time.

Ross and his marketing team had not been too happy with the content on the site and the app. Stuart had influenced a fair amount of it; it was transactional and price focused with little to no tie-in with the brand and what it was trying to achieve. Truth be told, he had the numbers that supported what they said. There was a higher percentage of visitors who left the site within a minute of getting there when the brand campaign was on. There were elaborate TikTok influencer campaigns about destinations that were missing any supporting content on the site. Stuart was worried about site-loading time; he wanted his site to be no-frills and easy to navigate. All he cared about was optimizing price per seat and getting conversions. He prided himself on his team's ability to maximize margin for the airline. Thankfully the IT team was on his side.

It had become a zero-sum game. If the airline's top management concluded that building a brand was necessary to get new people in, he would lose budget. His investments in infrastructure might get questioned and his generative AI bets would never take off the ground. He thought long and hard before deciding to send an email to his ally. He asked for a breakfast meeting the next morning with Sabiha Singhal, the long-term CFO of the airline and someone the board had immense trust in. Surely, she would understand.

## The Meeting

It was a small room with a round table that could accommodate five people. *Richard* liked it that way. He wanted to look into the eyes of everyone in the room to see if there was fear or confidence in them as they spoke. He was a big believer in nonverbal communication and was always prepared to convey the right mood through choices of his body and eye movement. It was known in the corridors of the airline that how you behaved got you more marks with Richard than what you said.

Richard was under the microscope by the board. He had overestimated the growth rate of the airline for the year, a deliberate move on his part. It was as if by making the claim the rest of the organization would pony up and follow him to create the results he wanted. But Sabiha, with whom he had a weird love–hate relationship, had probably made it known to the board that she did not think the numbers were achievable. It made him want to gnash his teeth.

During a transformation, one had to make the leap. And numbers never supported making big leaps; it was skill, talent, and magic of a product that helped make it happen. But number-oriented accountants had torpedoed so many such leaps; even the great Steve Jobs had been a victim. Richard pulled his thoughts away from finance and focused on Ross, who had just presented a summary of the campaign and had come to a slide called Implications.

He could read the tension in the room; after all, this was his thing. Ross had flipped through the campaign achievement slides briskly without any claims of great work. Stuart had been sitting straight through, his face an inscrutable mask, but Richard could sense the displeasure and dislike for Ross behind his neutral gaze. Sarah was fidgeting; she was stressed, and he could understand why. She was caught between a rock and a hard place, and both were in the room. Only Sabiha was relaxed; she had her legs crossed and had a calm demeanor about her as if she could not be rushed. Or as someone who already knew the outcome.

It was time for him to step in.

"Before we go ahead with implications, could I get a few things clear in my head?"

"Sure," Ross responded. He had been expecting an intervention.

"In effect, what you're telling me is that we increased our budget by roughly 10 percent and sold an incremental 12 percent seats over the same period. Brand favorability scores increased by 23 percent despite #AirlineGate and some of that translated into more seats being sold to nonleisure customers. Our average yield on our new business-class seats was better than expected, but we underdelivered on the budget segment—ostensible reason being crippling price wars. We didn't hit our goal of growing plane load factor by 17 percent. Take me through why we didn't hit our goals. Let's just talk."

He could notice Sabiha's interest perk up. At least he had shattered her sense of calm.

"Well," began Ross, assuming he was expected to go first. "We did a great job of reaching people who hadn't flown with us before. Our reach for this campaign was 35 percent higher than that of our last one. Not only did we reach more people, but we also reached a different set of people. We just didn't convert enough of them to get the growth we wanted. Not to mention, the social media backlash didn't help in promoting our brand."

"Why?"

There it was, the question Ross had been dreading all weekend and all of last night. The one for which he had a long answer but one that involved becoming transparent and setting out the issues for all to see. He shifted in his chair perceptibly, not unnoticed by Richard.

But he didn't get a chance to respond first.

"Could it be because the audiences we were trying to influence were not the people we should have gone after in the first place?" Sabiha had beaten him to it. He could feel an axe dangling above him.

*Authorial Intrusion: This is a classic moment that illustrates that the presence of data does not make decisions logical. The reality was that the audience segments touted by the agency and supported by Ross had not been used. They were watered down and calibrated to suit Stuart's beliefs. The person who had negotiated this was Sarah, a person on Ross's team. If Ross came out and suggested that the new audiences had not been used, attention would turn to Stuart but also to Sarah. It wasn't fair to her; she had kept him apprised, and he had decided to go ahead with it to win Stuart's approval. If he said that the new audiences did work, then he would have to quote the lack of content and get into a direct battle with Stuart, which might not lead to a very productive conversation. A veteran leader, Ross wanted to get to the heart of the problem without letting this discussion spiral into personalities and name-calling.*

*Authorial Intrusion: A point about reach: Ross was giving a general mainstream media reach number that was estimated. It wasn't deterministic and did not involve any reach garnered by any of Stuart's campaigns.*

"I don't think we were prepared for the new audiences. We didn't have content that supported what they were looking for, and our conversion rates on them weren't great. But they did engage with us on our messaging. Our click-through rates to our site were the best we have ever seen. The biggest variable driving traffic though was Time in View. The more people saw our commercials for a longer time, the more they decided to come check us out. We just weren't ready for them." Sarah had spoken in a clear steady voice; she had understood

Ross's hesitation and, being the analytics person, had decided that it was time they looked at facts. Ross would have given her a big hug and any increase she asked for at that moment.

"Why were we not prepared? Stuart, did we not have the right landing pages?" Richard interrupted with his *Why* question again.

Richard could notice Stuart's slight lack of enthusiasm in jumping into this debate. Classic passive–aggressive mentality, he thought as he watched Stuart shuffle through his papers.

"I wouldn't characterize it that way. There was content for them, it just wasn't as rosy or animation heavy as the ads were because we have a load limitation set by IT. We measure ourselves on time taken to buy a ticket online. Customers who come to our site expect to see prices quickly so they can make decisions. Besides, one could also argue that the people who bounced quickly were probably looking to understand the destination more rather than buy a ticket. And we have been clear that our site is just another booking engine. Perhaps we should have set aside a budget for a separate site that just focused on this content you need with a link to our booking engine."

"We did, remember? And then we gave you the budget to keep sales up," retorted Ross, his voice going up just a small notch.

"And it did deliver. I can see that our direct sales has never been stronger. In fact, we have dropped our cost per acquisition by 8 percent," Sabiha chimed in.

*Ah,* thought Richard, *I see.* He understood Sabiha's earlier calm now.

"Sarah, we spoke about full funnel models the last time we met. I'm sure you did a postmortem on this one. What did we find?"

"When the brand campaign budget declined after the initial burst, we saw a drop in site and app traffic. Brand favorability did not translate into increased conversions. It did spark more social conversations and, in fact, was one of the main reasons that the backlash did not impact our sales that much. We stayed on air for some time instead of disappearing. Our conversions of those who continued to turn up at our site was at the same rate as before, but the spike wasn't there. In fact, if our brand campaign had led to the same conversion rate we normally have, we would have crushed it."

"I'd love to take a look at the model." Richard could look at Stuart, who was almost close to sneering. He reminded him of his pet dog Rocky, who could be quite docile through the day but snarl and bare his teeth at another dog that threatened his fiefdom.

"I think it would be a good idea to share that model with Stuart," Sabiha chipped in.

"I don't think we need to do that. Let's get Nielsen and a couple of other research folks in. Sarah, run an RFP and let's identify someone who could be an effective third party that does this under your supervision. We could then use their output to tie everyone's KPIs in, including that of our agency. I know we haven't been big believers in copy pretesting but let's institute that as well. I'd like to see those copy test scores before we put them out. Also, I want us to relook at our audiences. And this time, Ross, once you're done with the work, I need you to take me through it in detail. Stuart, you will help Ross as much as you can. Great work in keeping the conversions going, but we are going to need more at the top for you to keep converting. Sabiha, let's discuss budgets tomorrow. I want to figure out where we can cut expenses to help get more people into our brand." Richard had authoritatively jumped in; he could see this meeting going off the rails.

There would be wheeling and dealing behind his back now. Heck, his own CFO would be right at it, and he knew certain board members who would be happy to help. But he was tired of following the old model. He needed to drive growth and that never came easy.

The meeting broke up with everyone licking their wounds and grateful for not having to go through a prolonged conversation that would have resulted in some honesty around the table. They could go back to playing chess.

## ME AGAIN

I have again crunched a number of different small meetings and conversations into a set of fewer dialogues and one meeting to dramatize the effect of certain behaviors and decisions. In most cases, there is death by a thousand cuts, whereby individuals and teams slowly lose sense of what they set out to do and end up grabbing at proxies that seem to indicate success. It's also not true to say that every single marketing campaign ends this way; there are usually a number of successes, but these successes do not necessarily translate to business success or a better customer experience.

I deliberately chose to not revisit the customer experience because the point has been made. People didn't love the site or app experience. Getting aligned across multiple departments is hard, impossible sometimes.

The CEO/CFO relationship is a deliberate provocation. It's a proxy for a cost versus value discussion. In some cases, the CFO ends up representing procurement, which is cost driven. It is not meant to indicate that all CFOs are focused on cost and all CEOs are focused on value. Often, they are not.

But in my experience, CFOs tend to prioritize cost reduction over other methods of driving business value when push comes to shove. That's just what they do, and while there might be exceptions, ask any CMO, and they'll bear me out in private. And unless the business makes an extra effort to figure out what works and what doesn't, it's quite easy for a CEO to accept his/her CFO's recommendation and focus on efficiency versus efficacy.

# CHAPTER SIX

## Fuck It Works! Part 1

As is evident from the previous chapters, a lack of alignment across the entire marketing ecosystem and perverse incentives have led to a significant gap between what matters versus what should truly matter. As I spoke to a number of people in the industry, I was struck by a couple of truths. The overwhelming majority acknowledge that there is a problem in marketing and advertising, that we are not in touch with people's expectations, and that if we did not resolve some of these issues, others would resolve them for us—and there is no guarantee that we would be able to live with the solution. The second truth was polarizing. There were some who were resigned to the situation and were content to blame the same ecosystem without hope of a solution and then there were others who were trying to break the mold.

It's these people and their efforts that lead me to believe that all is not lost … yet. There are examples of pathbreaking work that have the potential to become great advances, a break from the monotony of allowing false boundaries to restrict our expectations and ambitions and a sense of urgency driven by necessity. As with many human challenges, we seem to rise to the level of excellence and innovation only when these challenges become defining or when we are presented with binary moments around survival.

I decided to look for examples of such work driven by men and women who were trying to break paradigms and set new standards for success. In a way, it was a great experience for me to reconnect with some of the theory that drives many of our practices today and speak to people evolving them. It was also cathartic; I had lost touch with some of the fun and the science that drives thinking in the mad rush to meet numbers or get a deck done on time.

When I joined the industry, I was lucky to work with mentors who were crazy enough to challenge the status quo. They would turn up in the afternoon after a night of binge drinking and question all my thoughts and ideas for a pitch a day before the actual pitch. And I would rewrite the deck four hours before pitch time because we would have changed the entire approach of market prioritization, which would have an impact on all down-the-line elements including creative and media strategies.

I miss that sense of chaos and the desire to question conventional wisdom. So, I hunted for that in our industry. And I did find it.

The examples you will find here are by no means exhaustive, and I'm not going to reassure you that all these methods and approaches have worked or are likely to work, but they do offer a blueprint for what we must as an industry do in order to get our collective act together. There are a few criteria that I used to pick these: I wanted to capture horizontality, the ability to work across disconnected platforms or media to create a complete picture and improve the consumer or brand experience.

Granted, within each digital or technology platform, there is optimization and analytical work that are brilliant in scope and drive incredible results. But I deem that par for the course. If you had all that data, such as an Amazon or a Google, and couldn't pull off some of the stuff they do, then that's a fail as opposed to a WOW moment. The true WOW comes when platforms come together or brands innovate. It comes when models are challenged and proven to not work the way they are meant to, and brands make the leap with researchers to identify different ways of solving a problem.

And yes, there is AI. I consciously left AI out of the earlier chapters. Because in many cases, it is cited as a panacea for many ills. AI is the penthouse built on top of a house and if that house has shaky foundations, so does AI. But there are mechanisms by which AI can finally solve some knotty problems that have outlasted abilities of analytics products to solve.

So, for the next chapters, let's shun the sense of skepticism that I admit I've had a huge hand in creating and focus our attention on some pathbreaking work and theory that could help brands, the people who consume them, and the marketer who has spent the last decade or so wrapping her head around the acceleration of data and technology impact on her world.

## TV–Show Us the Way

TV advertising is the butt of many "informed" news pieces by the trade press. Linear TV advertising is in crisis, streaming is unprofitable (cue Bob Iger photo with shades and a white slightly ruffled shirt looking pensive), reports of ratings drops or cable cord cutters, layoffs at Warner Discovery CNN (couldn't make up my mind on how best to term them), perennial Nielsen gaffes (to read some of these pieces would suggest that Nielsen completely sucks), or new capabilities of AI-driven digital platforms dominate the news cycle. Yet, where exists crisis, chaos, and—my perennial favorite—desperation, there arises innovation pushed by forces that temporarily align.

If you peer under the hood, there isn't any rocket science in most of these stories. But it becomes stark when you see it from a different perspective. I plead the fifth on whether this is the truth, but let's say my doctor asks me to change my diet from my daily dose of sodas, chips, and burgers to a diet that is more organic, home cooked, and has less red meat. As a result, let's say that I actually follow this advice and start consuming avocado toast, acai bowls, and salads and skip sodas for water that has been collected from some pure mountain source, not to mention add in a gym workout or two.

It's guaranteed that my cost of living will go up. If I spent X on food, it's probably going to be 3X now. And the gains will probably become more apparent when I get tests done in a few months that demonstrate improvements at various levels.

If you only looked at cost of living, you would conclude that this was a failure and that the replacements had led to a deterioration in my living circumstances. If you started measuring calories or the level of sugar or cholesterol in my blood, you would come to a different conclusion. It seems so self-evident that I'm even thinking about deleting these paragraphs and sparing you agonizing truths.

But if we grasp this so easily, why do we not grasp the TV problem that is fairly similar? People have changed their behaviors; they are consuming from different platforms. Those platforms are more expensive to sustain like my new diet. However, they also present us with great opportunities: the ability to tell interactive targeted stories for example (reducing my cholesterol level). Yet we are stuck with metrics that don't make sense in this new world. Cost of delivery is the only metric that gets used. (Cost of food in my daily budget.)

Hence, the TV stations are producing great content that supposedly doesn't attract eyeballs as measured in traditional media, the new media like streaming have no benchmarks in this weird world and are forced to adhere to the economics of scale as if they were broadcast media, costs are spiraling upward because it becomes unsustainable, and a really poor ad experience is being thrust down people's throats in order to continue to fund expensive content the old-fashioned CPM way. (One of my favorite pastimes is to watch ads and guess which of my household attributes they used for targeting me. When I watch Hulu, it's confusing as heck. It's worse than watching linear TV, and that's saying something.)

You wouldn't accept it if I asked you to continue eating burgers with high cholesterol levels. Why do you accept an equivalent for your brands?

TV has had a measurement problem and continues to have one, and the reason for this problem's existence is not solely the often-demeaned TV station executives. It's that the rest of us are not willing to budge from valuing it the old-fashioned way. And we have taken too long to fix this problem. Between the measurement and research industries and the agency holdcos, we have made a right royal mess of it.

Meanwhile, here is what people say: Can you stop showing me the same ad in every break and boring me to death? (Fifty-nine percent of consumers polled who watch video content through streaming indicated that there are too many ads repeated during the same ad break or single episode according to Conviva's "State of Streaming Advertising 2021" as conducted by Dynata, June 15, 2021, and quoted by eMarketer.)[26]

But TV, or rather some broadcasters, have been looking to improve the balance between advertisers and consumers, whether it is in regulating ad loads or evolving targeting.

One of the people I've watched and worked with over the years who has been at the forefront of this change is Krishan Bhatia, ex-president and chief business officer at NBCUniversal. I started to

26 Schomer, accessed October 24, 2023.

discuss targeting with him around 2018 as NBC acquired Sky and its AdSmart platform.

Since then, Krishan has been driving the adoption of currencies closely tied to what advertisers value, which really depends on the way you target and measure.

The thesis was simple: if you know more about the types of consumers you're trying to reach as a brand and there are datasets that you can use in order to dimensionalize the attributes of those audiences, then more targeted segments can be created even in linear television that can get a higher concentration of the people that matter. Not only does the brand improve its efficacy but it also improves its efficiency because against the target audience that matters, its cost to reach that audience is lower than if a bad proxy had been used.

Bad proxies are a bane for marketing and are commonly found. Anyone who fights bad proxies sits in my good books.

This is why I picked the OpenAP effort and the Joint Industry Committee or JIC as the first examples of pathbreaking work that we must pay attention to and help support. OK, the JIC versus the MRC and its ills are well reported and it's quite possible that by the time this book makes it to print, both these ventures derail or are critiqued, but I still feel that TV is at least trying to get measurement right.

OpenAP focused on getting programmers together and JIC is currently focused on getting the rest of the industry and key stakeholders aligned. In other words, get your shit together first and then help others get their shit together.

It is a great blueprint for how horizontality should and could work.

## OPENAP/JIC

OpenAP began as a result of multiple broadcasters getting together and forming a consortium focused on standardizing audience targeting and cross-platform measurement practices. It was initially formed by Viacom, Fox, and Time Warner. While Warner has left post its sale by ATT, today the consortium includes NBC Universal, Univision, CBS, AMC Networks, and others like the Weather Channel. By the time this book releases in 2024, it's quite possible that more networks would have joined or at least that's my hope.

Could you imagine a consortium including Apple, Google, Meta, and Amazon working toward a common audience targeting and measurement platform?

The simplest way to understand OpenAP is a cross-platform data service that helps advertisers get access to publisher data, build their own solutions on top of them, and find the audiences they need.

The big issue facing the industry was different programmers using different approaches to reach specific segments. Also, siloed approaches don't scale, and unduplicated reach and frequency would become a casualty just as it is in today's digital ecosystem. OpenAP was designed to be a response to standardize inputs, outputs, and measurement, which allowed it to build a platform to allow more marketers to buy media against metrics that matter in a scaled fashion.

With the standardization done by OpenAP, there are common audience definitions across publishers, the dataset itself is cleansed, and both linear and digital get unified. Anyone who has tried to standardize taxonomies across campaigns and clients would appreciate this.

The solution is built on data clean rooms with Snowflake having invested in OpenAP in October 2022. As a partnership, that was a smart bet by the OpenAP team. Bad technology choices or lack of ability to build technical solutions often hinder many such efforts; getting someone proven in early solves that problem and builds trust in the solution.

So, what's a data clean room? I've defined this term before, but it bears repeating.

A physical clean room is a controlled space where control is exerted and rules are applied consistently to access documents, etc. There is a high degree of security and in a physical clean room used by labs, etc., there are no pollutants or outside particles allowed. A data clean room is modeled on this.

It's a controlled space where user data is anonymized, possibly aggregated, and matched with multiple sources. However, only agreed-upon elements of that dataset are allowed to be viewed or used for analytics or profiling by parties to the agreement. The key elements are making sure there is a common identifier that can match data and that the data is encrypted so that the underlying PII cannot be accessed.

But as my friend Brian Lesser, CEO of InfoSum, one of the foremost providers of data clean rooms, explains, "Instead of sending data over to us, we license our technology to you. And you use the technology through Bloom filters and other mechanisms that we have developed to match those audiences and run analytics without either party seeing those audiences or sending data to third-party identity systems."

Bloom filters are a probabilistic data structure that are used to figure out if an element belongs to a set or not. It won't tell you if an element is definitely a member of a set but it will definitely tell you if it's not. So, in this case, it helps identify audiences that are potentially members of both datasets that are getting matched.

It's an elegant solution that has been used by the digital platforms to grudgingly give access to aggregated data and provide environments where advertisers could bring their first-party data, combine it with aggregated data from the platforms, and either create better audience profiles or get better at measurement.

Some advertisers are looking to build their own clean rooms to help them manage cross-platform reach and frequency. As an added benefit, they do protect user privacy, help protect companies from privacy laws, and help get better solutions.

In an interview with Beet.tv, Abbey Thomas, CRO of OpenAP, mentioned the impending launch of a streaming data service in early 2024.[27]

I spoke with David Levy, CEO of OpenAP, in May 2023 about the journey he and his company have been through and the impending progress he expects to make. Even over Zoom, David seemed unflappable and collected; he didn't give any sign of what I'm sure are incredible pressures to get a new currency and measurement platform adopted across an often fractious industry. The more I spoke to him, the more I sensed calm.

He said, "Whereas a lot of the digital platforms look at data and privacy as a competitive advantage for their advertising products, I think most of the TV programmers are thinking about collaboration to bring the same kind of scale to solutions that some of these social and digital platforms can, making them more competitive as a whole."

One of the main objectives of OpenAP is to find a bridge between the traditional panel-dominated approach of Nielsen and the like, which has for years been the standard bearer of TV measurement, and big data or census-level data about viewership habits, behaviors, and other attributes of populations.

David shared that "to do this, we're having to pull together census-level data across all the programmers in a privacy-centric way without

---

27 https://www.beet.tv/2023/08/big-data-new-currencies-clean-rooms-a-peek-inside-openaps-future.html.

them having to actually give up their data or pass their data but resolve it to a common identity framework. And then have a privacy and clean room framework, where agencies can create their own audiences in a sandbox and be able to see where those audiences are viewing content or bringing in their own measurement solutions to produce either pre-campaign, mid-campaign, or post-campaign measurement insights that can improve the performance of a campaign."

That's a heck of a challenge, unifying multiple content creators behind a single set of standards while keeping each constituent happy.

But getting panel and big data together is a necessity. Or is it? I spoke to Radha, chief research and analytics officer at CBS, someone whom I've known and respected for quite some time. The question that I always used to confront in creating audience solutions was choosing between big data and legacy panels.

One of the points she made was interesting. "There is a fair amount of over-the-air TV viewing in certain communities like Asians and Hispanics. Some households have cable boxes and a smart TV. Therefore, just using big data might make sense for a marketer looking to close the loop with purchase data, but if you're looking to grow the business, you want to reach African Americans, Asians, and Hispanics who may not be on cable boxes at all."

(Over-the-air is using antennas to grab signals without needing a cable box or an internet connection. Yup, it still exists. In fact, over eighteen million households or roughly 15 percent of the US population are still using "rabbit ears."[28])

---

28 Jon Lafayette, "Nielson Sees Uptick in Over-the-Air Households," April 21, 2022, accessed October 1, 2023, https://www.nexttv.com/news/nielsen-sees-uptick-in-over-the-air-households#:~:text=18.6%20million%20homes%20using%20antennas%2C%20or%2015%25%20of%20the%20U.S.&text=Rabbit%20ears%20are%20multiplying.,a%20new%20report%20from%20Nielsen.

In any such solution, therefore, pragmatism has to be a component. Which is why the system is designed to allow for multiple measurement providers, multiple agencies to build their own products atop what is being provided for planning and measurement purposes, and even multiple identity mechanisms.

Levy shared, "We are looking to have OpenAP be the identity mechanism for cross-platform television targeting and measurement. That might mean that we use LiveRamp on one campaign, Transunion on another, we could use our proprietary ID spine, or Cadent but the process remains consistent."

Key stakeholders have plenty of reasons to be happy. OpenAP has become a scaled business and is rumored to be contributing $100 million plus to each of the programmers.

While it seems chaotic and I'm sure there will be teething troubles along the way, the US market does not lend itself to single-provider solutions such as in the United Kingdom or other smaller markets. Ultimately only a balance between a centralized solution that offers a framework with different embedded or attached solutions will work no matter how messy it becomes.

The need to have multiple stakeholders aligned and adopting such standards is the impetus behind the JIC. Most cross-industry initiatives usually die a painful death by a thousand viewpoints and a hodgepodge of self-interests. It's been one of the reasons why regulators and policy wonks don't accept what our industry trade bodies recommend at face value unlike in other industries, such as telecom.

But the JIC feels different.

The JIC membership is half buyers and half sellers and is tasked with coming up with evaluation criteria that can help score and certify whether a measurement company can provide solutions. It recognizes that measurement and currency, in particular, needs to move from a single provider to a multiprovider environment.

As is the norm, even well-meaning initiatives in our industry cannot gain consensus because, of course, we have our own points of view. Nielsen has stood out and criticized the whole process and decided to not participate.

It's really poor form in my opinion. First you screw up in not keeping in touch with consumer habits and technologies, then you screw up with weak samples and not keeping up to your own standards during COVID, and now you don't want to participate in probably one of the only industry bodies that is actually making progress? Recipe for growth.

The JIC instituted a request for information (RFI) framework that evaluated measurement providers on cross-platform capability, big data, tech and infrastructure, interoperability, privacy, transparency, governance, cross-media transparency, and planning and optimization. These are all concerns for the entire industry and I love the fact that there is work toward addressing the cross-platform demon in the room.

## EDO—TV MEASUREMENT INNOVATION

I chose a different approach to write a book about data. Even though I've spent a lot of time with data and its applications, I chose to speak to a wide cross-section of the industry to refresh myself, learn, and understand where some of the magic existed. And meeting Kevin Krim, president and CEO of EDO Inc., was one of the advantages of this method. If you want to understand modeling and its impact without having to go through the detail, you should speak to Krim. Chances are though that if you're a reasonably senior marketer, you have met him. I decided to feature EDO because their story and what they do is a microcosm of the challenges in measurement and potential innovations that could end up resolving them.

EDO was founded in 2015 by Edward Norton (yes, the actor) and Daniel Nadler to fix issues with linear TV measurement. Given Edward's background, initial focus was the entertainment industry. But over time EDO has transformed into a full-blown measurement company focused on evaluating TV campaigns across linear and streaming platforms by using smart TV data, Google Trends, and other sources to connect offline behaviors to online search patterns.

Kevin cut his teeth in the TV measurement industry first with Bloomberg and then with CNBC, both of which had great content, which they believed was not being fairly represented in Nielsen data. His frustration with Nielsen led him to explore alternative ways of accounting for audience impact. He landed on using spikes in search traffic to measure the impact of TV advertising; this wasn't very new as an idea but had rarely been perfected and hardly used except to wow clients in pitches. OK, that was a bit cynical, but I've seen enough agency pitch decks where ideas go to die. But Kevin and his team gave this idea structure and rigor.

According to Kevin, "Search accurately reflects consumer intent even if the nature of search is changing. And linear TV generates a large volume of viewership data. It is possible to spot spikes in search traffic and link them to TV ad viewership."

There is enough evidence that clearly demonstrates the ability of Share of Search (SOS) of a brand to predict the direction of its Share of Market (SOM). In most cases, brands still tend to look at the relationship between Share of Voice (SOV) and SOM, a legacy construct that has probably outlived its use. The theory has been that a high SOV implies that because you outshout your competitors, you're likely to achieve greater reach and awareness that translates to greater market share.

But it doesn't take into account the quality of the SOV. Not all ad placements are the same, and they drive different outcomes. But the relationship between SOS and SOM is clear.

The Institute of Practitioners in Advertising (IPA) group in the United Kingdom, led by Les Binet, an awarded researcher and ace econometrist, and EDO conducted an analysis of multiple brands (across twelve categories) in various countries (seven) to identify the linkage between SOS and SOM.[29]

Here is what they found. SOS correlates closely with SOM (83 percent). This was found to be true across categories: luxury auto (90 percent), non-luxury auto (92 percent), restaurants (96 percent), and CPG (85 percent).

Second, and more interestingly, excess SOS predicts SOM growth. Take the case of the auto and home insurance industry in the United States. In 2016, State Farm had the SOM at less than 30 percent, while its SOS was closer to 20 percent. Progressive showed the opposite trend. Over the next five years, State Farm lost both SOS and SOM while Progressive gained in both.

You didn't really need audience data to arrive at this, did you?

Getting this to work, though, is hard work and requires a level of modeling expertise and sheer grunt work to cleanse data. It was the main reason that most attempts to connect these two data sources hadn't scaled well.

The starting point of getting search data at a minute-by-minute level was relatively easy; it was available through Google Trends, although the EDO team had to do a fair amount of parsing and

---

29 EDO.com, "Share of Seach Predicts Market Share Growth," accessed October 13, 2023, https://landing.edo.com/share-of-search-predicts-market-share-growth.

cleansing to make it usable. Connecting this to TV ad times was a bit trickier.

EDO built its own TV ad monitoring service, leveraging data centers to DVR all national TV. They then ran algorithms on the database to match audio and recognize national versus local channels. Machine learning and the arrival of the Cloud helped accelerate this a fair bit.

On the other hand, they also had to collect outcome data for brands, searches, website visits, downloads, etc., before they could attempt a match. They would definitely see spikes in search traffic, in some cases instantly as with NFL games and in other cases very fleeting ones. The trick was to arrive at a true baseline before being able to arrive at spikes.

Arriving at a true baseline needs a fair amount of understanding of variables, such as seasonality. During shopping season, for example, there are a fair number of clicks on e-commerce ads or traffic to e-commerce websites that is organic; a spike needs to produce results that rise above the organic baseline. Accuracy of the baseline is critical to determining success.

As the years passed, EDO collected data for multiple brands, allowing it to build a robust understanding of some of these variables. And none of this is PII.

For the entertainment or auto business, where the creative messaging mattered, this framework allowed EDO to do a deep dive on what worked and what didn't. This was just linear TV though. Streaming posed a completely different challenge.

Streaming TV has multiple sources of collecting data, both viewership and household demographics and others. The most obvious one, in other words, the apps on a TV, are ruled out. Most of the big streaming platforms have deals with TV manufacturers that prevent the manufacturer from allowing any data to be collected through the app. It started with Netflix, and now pretty much everyone does it.

Set top box and ad server data are not very reliable, though they do provide more information about the actual media being watched on the set. The strongest source is the smart TV itself, and most of the data comes from manufacturers like Vizio. And unless one has special permissions from viewers, a TV can only collect limited information, such as viewing patterns. It results in what Kevin coined as "Swiss cheese full of gaps."

To connect to outcomes, one needs Identity, a mechanism to connect households to the outcomes generated, often an IP address.

Where EDO went a step above was in stitching together multiple aggregate signals to identify relationships accurately. Between the TV sets, publishers, and the ad servers, EDO had answers to questions like what was being consumed, who saw the ad, and where they saw it. In order to get the behaviors and outcomes data, EDO relied on scaled panels of consumer behavior data to create a micro-cohort-based model.

Yup, I'm stopping; let's unpack this. Micro-cohorts are small groups of variables, in this case ad impressions clustered by time and zip code: for example, all those who saw the ad in NY 10001 between one and one-thirty in the afternoon to be matched with panel data of behaviors like downloads, searches, etc. Post that, there is a multi-touch attribution model built to map the relationships driving the behavior. This would allow a marketer to know what creative messages and in what media drove a consumer to behave in a certain way.

Easy, right?

The next step is to ingest first-party data from brands and try to connect them with aggregate panels and smart TV data to then connect the *who* to the behaviors and outcomes brands seek.

This is a classic example of the forest–tree distinction I've talked about in the past. You may not know which household did what, but if used well, this approach can create enough and more value for marketers to assess the value of their buys.

Trust me, many claim they can do this or that they do this already but very few can do it with rigor, discipline, and accuracy.

Why is this TV stuff so special anyway?

Horizontal effort and a drive to tie what once used to be a large expense to business outcomes makes this a great blueprint to follow. Not to mention, this effort could widen to encompass more players if marketers got behind it wholeheartedly. Laws and policies are all great, but standards are what ultimately make them real. And making standards is never easy. This effort by the TV industry across multiple players deserves support, and it's going to be very interesting to see how it progresses. There are clear issues cropping up with the VAB or Video Advertising Bureau not agreeing with the ANA's approach to Google and Meta on video measurement.

I don't begrudge the walled gardens their data and the fact that they use it to further their own interests, but I think we have reached the tipping point of what people will accept, and it might be left to the old idiot box to show us how to do it well again. That is if we let the old idiot box do its stuff.

# CHAPTER SEVEN

## Fuck It Works! Part 2

I have deliberately tried very hard to stay away from AI in this book. For some, it is a magic elixir. The real deal. Others will tell you it's smoke and mirrors or snake oil. In an era when companies are desperately renaming their businesses or finding any way possible to make their business about AI, I wanted to not make this book about AI. Because AI, to me, is a penthouse built on a great foundation of good, clean data that is usable. And, if anything, by now this book should have disabused you of the notion that such good, clean data exists outside the walls of the big tech companies in marketing. And as the example of EDO suggests in the previous chapter, it is possible to get there, but there is a fair amount of preparation and curation of data involved that can be quite back-breaking at times.

Couple this with the planned opacity and degradation of digital signals from consumers driven by overzealous legislation and poor policies, and the Open Web won't have much to offer in a matter of years in terms of what is needed for attribution models and the like. That makes the job of training AI algorithms harder and curation even more critical to get the best out of them.

As is the norm in the industry, we have rushed forward to tout partnerships, strike deals, and talk up the potential of AI to drive efficacy and efficiency. My biggest concern is that when the solution isn't structured well and the science is questionable, we end up with a sharp focus on cost since it's one of the few variables with good clean data. We have to make sure that AI doesn't end up going the way that programmatic media buying went—a race to the bottom chased by opacity and fraud. I don't want to live through that hell again.

With generative AI popping its head, there is a prevalent belief that AI is now more accessible. It is and it isn't. And as with most industries, there are AI horror stories, and the one I'm going to talk about highlights perfectly well why it looks so easy to implement and why it's not.

One of my friends in the AdTech industry narrated this gem. A hotel chain decided to use its room pricing data to train AI to set future prices. It was a perfect case: significant volume of data, narrow use case, tightly defined outcomes needed. Hotel execs were surprised to see the algorithm throw up increasing prices over time. It didn't seem to make any sense.

Turns out that the dataset had suggested that as prices increased, room occupancy rates improved. The underlying data signal that was missing and one with which the algorithm was not armed was information about the occurrence of events and conferences. Hence, the causal link between the two was missed.

It seems blindingly obvious, but if we could miss variables in such tightly defined situations, imagine the mess we could end up with inaccurate data or worse miss relevant variables that would help complete a picture.

Let's nerd out a bit on AI. There are different ways by which AI gets classified: there is artificial narrow intelligence (ANI), artificial general intelligence (AGI), and artificial super intelligence (ASI) approaches that don't help us much because we are still in ANI. ANI allows for narrow tasks to be performed well, and AGI is what the likes of OpenAI are gunning for, where a task that a human can perform can also be done by AI. ASI is the area of sci-fi where AI becomes superior to humanity in its ability to think, learn, and do (HAL 9000 in the Kubrick classic, for example). I prefer the classifications of Reactive, Limited Memory, Theory of Mind, and Self-Aware. Again, for our purposes to do with marketing, applications remain in the first two groups at best.[30] The other two refer to the equivalent of ASI.

Reactive AI responds to a stimulus; it doesn't remember and it doesn't learn per se. It's given an input, and it spits out an output. It has been around for some time and most recommendation engines run based on these machine learning models. (I'm treating machine learning as a subset of AI.) Most modern marketing analytics models are based on this and will continue to exist since they do their tasks very well.

Limited memory approaches involve getting smarter as they receive more data to train on. Again, while this mimics the human brain to a limited fashion, there is no capacity for true learning. Past and present data are used to build experiential knowledge and power the algorithm. Image recognition would be an application.

AI does have the potential to remake our industry; the question is whether we will use it for the right reasons or focus on eliminating people who are supposed to come up with ideas. There are two areas of AI applications that I am really stoked about and hope that they come true. Because they could, together, address some of the fundamental problems with data-driven marketing and bring us back on track to

---

30 https://www.forbes.com/sites/cognitiveworld/2019/06/19/7-types-of-artificial-intelligence/?sh=68ab045233ee.

bothering about the right outcomes. And surprise, surprise, we might even be able to pull this off without abusing the rights of consumers.

The first application is focused on addressing the creative problem. Quality of advertising, or the creative as it's called, makes a big difference to efficacy or outcomes. There is research that shows that creative messaging is the second biggest driver of a brand's profitability, the first being size of the brand. (Source: Paul Dyson, founder of Accelero Consulting in a talk at Thinkbox in the United Kingdom. Papers relevant to the subject have been published on warc.com.) Targeting is way down the list near the bottom in terms of contribution to brand profitability. The traditional problem in digital media has been the mismatch between the cost of producing multiple messages fine-tuned to people's needs and the relatively cheap cost of getting exposures. This has resulted in messages that are not made relevant to groups of people—forget individuals. Pair that with media targeting that seeks to be hyper-targeted. The result is messages or ads that don't engage people or make them feel like they are getting a unique experience.

The second application is focused on solving for the disappearance of consumer signals either because of the walled gardens or because of regulation. The common understanding is that AI works when there is volume of data related to the task at hand, and that the more data you have, the more likely you are to be successful at AI, which to a large extent is true...if you're looking to solve immensely complex problems all at once. But is there an approach where AI can thrive with limited data? In fact, is there an approach where AI can limit collection of data and still achieve brand goals? We shall see.

## The Meta Approach—Why I Like It and Why You Should Too

Apple introduced its App Tracking Transparency or ATT in April 2021. It gave power to users to decide whether they wanted an app to track them or not by limiting access to the Identifier for Advertisers or IDFA. I won't go into motivations behind the approach or the benefits to users, but it did effectively hit the digital ad ecosystem and specifically Meta pretty hard. Meta, with apps like Facebook and Instagram, relied on the IDFA to build its network and connect behaviors online to the PII it collected from users. That effectively got degraded.

The solution that Meta has come up with is a very nifty use of AI that should give many CMOs and marketers hope. I'm not advocating for Meta as much as I'm advocating for the AI approach that they have used. By building a platform that leverages AI to build messaging for advertisers based on their objectives plus more limited use of granular data, Meta has allowed for live optimization on the creative front to substitute for the loss of individual data gleaned from Apple devices. If this doesn't supplement the research mentioned above, I don't know what does.

By rotating through clusters of creatives and understanding response rates from users, an algorithm can predict what a creative needs to have in order to drive success, and even if it is linked to groups of users or cohorts, it is very effective. Dare I say it, it's almost a *TikTokian* way of solving the problem. TikTok uses AI to predict videos that are likely to get your attention by observing your every behavior as opposed to tracking you across sites. OK, that's a very big generalization, and I'm sure there is more to it than that. But if you substitute user-generated videos for ads and follow the same process, your monetization engine is alive. The signals coming from Apple devices can be effectively replaced over time.

The only hindrance to the above is computing power. You need a lot of it to do this with multiple users in so many different countries across languages, creative types, and content. My guess is that the layoffs from Meta helped direct investment to computing power.

The lesson between the research and Meta's use of AI is this: don't look at the degradation of individual data as an impediment to driving growth effectively using digital channels. In fact, by focusing on optimizing messaging, there are bigger gains to be made than pure media optimization. By changing the variable that gets evaluated, you can get around the loss of signals in other variables that are under the regulatory scanner. And even on media optimization, there are solutions to get around the loss of signals.

Most brands have either a desire or some form of first-party data collection project going on with tons of consultants and advisers involved. Some companies have multiples of smaller datasets sitting in different parts of the organization and are focused on consolidating them to drive scale with the belief that it will give them more insight and feed their own AI models. However, there might be approaches that could help brands leapfrog the need to build large datasets. Large is great, but sometimes you can thrive with so-so.

## Synthetic Is the Way to Go and Other Approaches

Let's take a nightmare scenario, which might actually be closer to reality than we think. Let's assume that, taking a cue from the California (Delete) bill, multiple states in the United States have made it easy for people to get themselves off data broker lists. Coupled with moves from Google and others, signals available in a third-party setting would have deteriorated. Previously, if census-level databases had information about three hundred million Americans, that will now go down to, let's say, five million. (I'm just picking a number; it could be higher or lower than this.) In a number of cases, there are panels and other sources of information that exist, but they cannot rival the scale of the national databases that existed before.

The only ones with data at scale are the big walled gardens and to a limited extent entertainment (Disney, Netflix, NBC, etc.) sectors. Does this set us back in our ability to have control over the way data and analytics can be used to grow brands? I posit that brands can, through innovative uses of AI like those highlighted above and others, still retain control over their future.

I spoke to my friend Ian Johnson about this very problem. We have five million Americans whose records are available. There are two preconditions according to Ian that must be adhered to: First, everything that we have known about the three hundred million needs to be known about the five million. And second, the five million must be statistically relevant compared to the total population. This will impact brands that are looking to work with smaller audiences or segments, especially in luxury categories.

In order to build data, the effort needs to focus on behaviors that matter, for example, striking deals with partner media to understand media behavior that can be used to power a brand's algorithm. This can also be done with retail media partners. Using clean rooms, one can get access to aggregate data and as long as the behaviors are being modeled on cohorts or aggregates, the AI gets trained. The same can be replicated with panel data. It will take time and effort to train the AI, but it would be the only way you can leverage your own algorithm that takes into account your business model and data and connects it to the outside world.

Few-shot learning techniques in machine learning can be used where training datasets are limited. Instead of using large datasets that allow the machine to learn, one uses limited but valuable datasets to learn combined with human inputs. Part of the reason why AI requires large datasets is because it takes a longer process to arrive at conclusions than humans do. We tend to use intuition or reasoning better with smaller datasets. Few-shot learning or low-shot learning is apparently great for math applications, great news for our models. Granted that some of these models need to be pretrained, but there are tons of small companies working on making these available.

Once the AI gets trained, it can create synthetic data to cover for any gaps in data collection or if there is a need to increase the volume of data for a use case. That would help create propensity models that are not as accurate as the ones you had before but are definitely more valuable than what you would be left with in our nightmare scenario.

For certain categories, like the financial sector, automobiles, health, and direct-to-consumer initiatives, this would pay off. If you're not in a sector that relied on proprietary data or models in the past to build a brand or drive growth, you may decide to outsource this to the platforms or OpenAI.

In fact, if you are a brand in any of those areas mentioned previously, you should be training your own AI on your existing data signals so that it can learn now when the knowledge exists. You will have to change your privacy policy and let people know about their data use case, but that's still preferable to building afresh in the future.

The true value of AI lies in its ability to (a) fill gaps created in datasets, which allows for model accuracy, and (b) become a true source of intelligence sitting atop multiple smaller systems that are throwing up seemingly disparate data or insights. It's highly unlikely that a common standard that allows data to pass between platforms owned by different entities is ever going to come.

Having direct data relationships with the walled gardens and the likes of OpenAP can allow your AI to train on aggregate data and learn patterns of behavior as well as connections to outcomes. Add in the creative approach like Meta and you might just realize that you didn't need data on the three hundred million Americans in the first place. AI is the only hope for marketers that intelligence can be garnered and put to use even in a fragmented media and data scenario powered by well-meaning but faulty regulations. That is if we don't all focus on cost-cutting efforts first and create programmatic apocalypse 2.0.

## THE MOVABLE MIDDLE GROWTH FRAMEWORK (MMGF)

I loved, loved, loved researching, interviewing, and writing this section. Of all the awesome work going on around marketing, this was one that had all the ingredients of strong intellect-based discussions and strategizing about using data to prove/disprove a hypothesis. Best of all, while there is a fair amount of math involved, the concept itself is so simple that once you read about the conclusions, you may wonder why we didn't follow some of this logic. And this also highlights one of the themes of this book: we are in many cases missing the forests for the trees and are hostage to legacies and proxies that we need to free ourselves from.

To dive into the world of growth models, I decided to begin by talking to Greg Stuart, CEO of the MMA, a trade body that is now focused on research that helps establish what drives or doesn't drive marketing impact. It used to be the Mobile Marketing Association, but Greg has broadened its perspective, which shows in the quality and depth of the MMA's work.

Greg's been around the block for some time now; he was the CEO of the IAB, has worked in the agency and media publishing space, and has written a book, *What Sticks: Why Most Advertising Fails and How to Guarantee Yours Succeeds*. One of the reasons I value Greg and his opinions is because the CMO is his most important and main client. And what matters to a C MO matters to him; unlike others, he cannot afford to have conflicts of interest.

I asked Greg about his thoughts on the state of data-driven marketing. We began with how data was not really a thing while personalization was and agreed that return on advertising spend (ROAS) was most important. And then I asked a question about segmentation and audiences and off we went to the races.

Let's get a few definitions and background out of the way. *Audiences* and *segmentation* are two words you've probably heard a lot about; the two are different even though in many cases they get used interchangeably. Audiences are groups of people who share similar characteristics; they could be demographic, attitudinal, behavioral, or purchase based. In many ways, a segmentation would have big overlaps with the definition of audiences. But there is one big difference. While segmenting, people get grouped into mutually exhaustive and exclusive segments, but audiences allow for the same people to be classified differently. This is important because, too often, audience profiling and creation is seen as a substitute for segmentation or, even worse, the two remain unconnected concepts in a marketing ecosystem for a brand.

The next thing to keep in mind is that growth frameworks and frequency of exposure frameworks have existed for a long time. There is the Byron Sharp Model, Peter Fader with Customer Centricity, and Les Binets. While each had differences and addressed problems differently, Byron Sharp is focused on making sure a brand reaches as many people as possible without bunching exposures together.[31] Peter Fader with his thoughts on the most valuable consumers and whether they should be the focus of a brand; and Les Binets with his thoughts on long-term and short-term brand-building approaches—*and* there is one common element across them.[32] All quibbles aside, they are based on reach. If you focus on just your customers, the thinking goes you won't grow market share. And market share growth is what drives long-term success of your brand. You reach more people, you get growth. And if you reach them over time in a steady drip, you maximize your opportunity to reach as many potential shoppers as possible.

This is accepted thinking across the marketing world and has been for quite some time. The entire media model is built around scale based on the idea that reach is important for driving market share growth. And the new performance models that have come about in the digital age have, after an interesting beginning, defaulted to reach. Get more impressions at a cheap rate and you have better chances of growing your brand or getting results. Volumes of impressions and clicks and other metrics have been subsumed by reach.

Let's now get back to Greg and a new model that he and the MMA call the Movable Middle Growth Framework.

Greg explained it to me using a simple analogy. In the world of coffee, let's say there are two brands: Starbucks and Dunkin'. There are three types of consumers: those who swear by Starbucks, those who

---

31 https://www.warc.com/content/feed/prof-byron-sharp-criticises-attention-metrics-argues-for-always-on-reach/en-GB/7144.

32 https://www.warc.com/newsandopinion/opinion/effectiveness-in-the-digital-age-insights-from-les-binet/en-gb/2411.

swear by Dunkin', and those who are willing to switch. The switchers might have preferences for one brand or the other, but they will still switch sometimes because they found some part of the other brand appealing in that moment.

A reach-based model would suggest that if either brand wanted to grow its share, it had to appeal to everyone. You do not want to lose your own consumers and you want to attract consumers of the other brand. Let's assume there is no product innovation that is going to make one brand superior to the other. Greg's argument is that marketers are arrogant to believe that advertising and marketing efforts can convince anyone to trade their preferences.

For a second, think about your own preferences. Pick the brands that you love the most and ask yourself if you would buy the competitor. If you were a diehard fan of the brand, you wouldn't. For many brands, you might feel differing levels of loyalty. It would be safe to say, I think, that brand lovers of Starbucks and Dunkin' are not likely to change their minds about the other brand because of a few ads or promotions.

That leaves the switchers; whether they are exactly 50/50 or at some range can be calibrated, but these are consumers who seek new experiences or flavors and are willing to switch. It would be a waste of resources to go after people who wouldn't be caught dead in a Starbucks or a Dunkin'. (There are such people apparently!)

This model has parallels with the way Billy Beane, the Oakland A's manager, changed baseball. It comes down to the metrics we value and the decisions we take basis those metrics. Billy asked the question around what was valuable or what was being bought. In this model, we are reframing the question around who is more valuable to a brand. The brand switchers, the ones who are actually persuadable, the *Movable Middles,* are the most valuable segment.

As an aside, I asked Billy Beane to address my data and technology team; yes, I have read the book and seen the movie. But to be in the room when Billy explains sabermetrics should be on a data fan's bucket list.

Greg connected me to Joel Rubinson, the man behind the model. And speaking to him was another treat. Joel is a researcher, is a specialist at multi-touch attribution (he serves as the MMA's expert on the subject), was the former chief research officer of the Advertising Research Foundation, and is currently the president of Rubinson Partners focused on consulting for marketers. One of the reasons I love Joel: he doesn't mince his words.

Joel thinks that there are three challenges that prevent most marketers from being successful. The first one relates to the data pipes being set up so that the information needed is accurately captured and made available for analytics. I can't argue with him on this; I've seen too many companies where data collection and application resemble a bull in a china shop. The second challenge relates to having what Joel calls "the right mental model." You could have ideas that are harmful. He cites an example of an automobile manufacturer who decided to target his competitor's customers as a conquest mechanism. "It's the stupidest example of targeting. If they are customers of the other brand, they are not going to necessarily switch and buy you."

The third challenge relates to looking at the wrong approach: reach is all that matters, and you don't need targeting. (I would add that bad approaches to targeting are equal to no targeting at all.)

What Joel found was that instead of looking for demographic, attitudinal, or other sources of data, you should look for propensity to buy a brand and marry that with ad exposure. Here is where math comes in, and in the interest of making sure that your eyes don't glaze over and I lose you, I'm going to do my best to keep it simple. I should mention that Joel and the MMA had a number of partners including multiple brands, UCLA, and Neustar (now bought by Transunion) from a data perspective and others to prove or disprove the model.

It goes like this: Most consumers of a category are either very low or unresponsive to a brand's advertising and some are on the other end—they are highly loyal. If you mapped ad response and initial purchase probability, you would get a beta distribution. What the fuck is that? Good question. A beta distribution is a probability distribution of probabilities. An easier way of understanding it is a method to model probabilities in different scenarios. In this case, we are looking to model ad response to an initial purchase probability. Because it models a probability, your range is set between 0 and 1 or you could refer to it in percentages.

We are effectively trying to figure out the lift in purchase probability across consumers from Low Responsives to High Loyals. What Joel found was that consumers in the middle who had an initial purchase probability from 30 to 70 percent had a 5-times responsiveness to ads. Responsiveness is defined as lift in purchase probability. In simpler words, if you marketed to the Movable Middles, your ads had a 5-times response rate. (If you are interested in knowing, this was arrived at using the Logit model. You can visit the link in the footnote for the explanation from Joel himself.[33])

If you put the two together, the distribution of the category buyers across their initial purchase probabilities with the ad response lift in purchase, you will see that way too much money is being wasted on people who are unlikely to respond to a brand's ads, while focusing on the movable middle gets you greater ROAS.

Here is the fallacy of reach-based planning. If 80 percent of category buyers on average—and this can change by category or brand

---

33 https://www.mmaglobal.com/movable-middles.

across Low Unresponsives and High Loyals—don't respond to your advertising, then by chasing everyone, there is a fair chance that most of your spend is a waste. As Joel explains, "The movable middle is hyper-responsive to advertising. Instead of being obsessed with reach, obsess over hyper-responsiveness."

This begs the questions, how do you reconcile audience with segments, and how do you adjust your targeting and media strategies to go after the Movable Middles? Joel elaborates that you have to target audiences where most of a brand's movable middle segment is located. This does question much of the audience creation work that goes on. It isn't the approach as much as the overall strategy used. Focusing spend on audiences who are less likely to be Movable Middles is going to get fewer business results even if they might be cheaper to find and address.

There is then the challenge of the walled gardens. Many of them offer self-service prepackaged audiences (which Joel calls "bullshit"). In other words, there is not going to be a plan that offers addressability only for those who are Movable Middles. And in fact, there shouldn't be either. Because we might think of High Loyals or heavy buyers to be in the bag, but chances are they are probably heavy buyers of other brands too. So, not all the spillover is bad.

The other impact of this approach is that it doesn't favor digital media much because of the aforementioned point on walled gardens. The likes of Amazon and others can and are probably using models such as these to get better returns; the poor marketer doesn't get all the benefits. Shopper data and connected TV, though, seem like a great combination for finding opportunities to target Movable Middles.

One of the brands that participated in the study with Joel and the MMA was Ally Financial (850,000 consumers in the dataset), and I caught up with Andrea Brimmer, its CMO, to talk about the work and what her impressions were. (As an aside, if you didn't know, women's sports is a passion for her and she has done a lot to use her influence to get women's sports, such as soccer, more support. I hear she was an amazing soccer player herself!)

"Two years ago, I would have said that a reach-based model was the way to go to market. In our category like banking, it's really hard to get someone to switch. Movable Middles are six times more likely to open an account, are 87 percent more efficient to acquire, and are predisposed to expand their relationship with us at a far higher rate than others."

I asked her about what that meant for messaging. "A steady diet of brand-oriented communication is needed. If you only use performance messaging, you will convert sooner, they won't stay, and there is no annuity in having them relative to their lifetime value."

In terms of reach-based and movable middle-based approaches, she said, "It's not an either/or. It's both. Demand creation can only come from making people fall in love with the brand."

So why is reach such a big draw? Simplicity. Reach is simple. As Einstein said, *Everything should be made simple, not simpler*. Some justification that is easy to understand makes it easier for others to accept. And some justification accepted by others is safe. Safe and simple won't get you fired. No one will fire you from moving your budget from a click-through rate of 0.04 percent to 0.2 percent.

I have heard this sentiment about not wanting to get fired being a major reason for not experimenting with metrics or different models from various parts of the industry.

I'll end with Joel's words, which really stuck a chord for me and can be factually examined. "Advertising can be a profit generator. It is seen, though, as an expense, which is why in recession, ad budgets get cut. You wouldn't be cutting it if you knew the amount of growth it gave you. Would you shut your best-performing store during a recession?"

His recall of a comment made by one of his old clients was priceless. "Advertising doesn't drive sales. Sales drives advertising." When advertising is an expense, sales decide the amount that you can afford to spend.

I believe that what Andrea outlined as an approach is the way to go. Whether you're a new brand or product, whether you're in insurance or cars will all decide the strategy to be used and the right balance of each approach.

But MMGF is an elegant solution, backed by work on many brands whose case studies you can access on the MMA's website. And, most importantly, it challenges the status quo and offers an alternative to models that have unfortunately been used to justify a cost reduction regime that would make procurement happier than would a CEO.

## Ethics: We Are All Ethical until We Are Not

Through my career across twenty-five years and three continents, I have completed assignments that, in some cases, troubled me and that in some cases I was too preoccupied to worry about. The common element between them was that they all posed ethical questions, and I had the wrong answers. If those decisions were taken by today's Arun Kumar, they would be very different.

In my fourth year of work in an Indian agency, I took on responsibilities to plan and buy media for a tobacco company. The product was not cigarettes, but a new range of fashion powered by retail stores. It was a big launch for a big advertiser, a launch of a surrogate brand, and I got lost in the work. I remember spending time reading the regulations for tobacco brand advertising at the time and working out ways by which I could get around them. Not because I loved cigarettes and wanted everyone to smoke, but between the adrenaline of such a big launch, the testosterone of my smoking colleagues, I forgot about what I cared for. When I think of those days, I am amazed with my own lack of empathy and utter stupidity in not thinking through my assignments. No one forced me to work on these assignments; I had the freedom to pick what I wanted to work on.

I have often tried to use the argument of *you were too young* to justify my decisions. But years later, I found myself helping another big international tobacco company in Jakarta. And this time, there was no surrogate to support; I worked on cigarettes in a developing country that couldn't afford the medical bills that smoking would entail. I was the only one in a meeting room with twenty-five people or so who didn't smoke firsthand as we debated media strategies. No excuse for that one.

Fast forward to the programmatic era. I watched my entire dream of creating an accountable media ecosystem go up in smoke as ad fraud killed the dream, one bot at a time. I sat in meetings where we would recommend programmatic budgets and I would mentally calculate the amount that I couldn't prevent from going to waste. *We have numbers to hit, families to feed, bonuses to give* went my refrain as I tried to shut these conversations in my mind and never spoke my mind to clients. My team and I tried ferociously to battle fraud, but there was only so much anyone could do then. Even today, made-for-advertising websites take a significant portion of media dollars in the programmatic ecosystem. The ANA reports are sobering reads.

Data and its usage are always hard; decisions around what sources to use and how to handle information about people can have a material impact on organizations. We could get a better match rate with this other data on-boarder, with whom we don't have a prior relationship; problem is by the time we dot the i's and cross the t's, the pitch is over. So why don't we just take our entire database and hand it to the on-boarder to do the match faster? I am not going to lose this goddamn pitch to Z and get stumped by privacy concerns! (This is a true incident I have observed with a competitor. We managed to win the business without making any data transfers, but to the client, it made no difference. Ethics and respect for privacy was not the reason we were chosen.)

Fossil fuel brands were another challenge. Do you work on them or not? A couple of years ago, my team did some great work for one such brand, and I sent a laudatory email to the company felicitating the team and appreciating the work. A member of the company reached out and raised a concern: How do you square your climate pledge and your appreciation of work done for a fossil fuel brand? Fuck, I hadn't thought about that. I just got into the work and loved it. I tried to dismiss the question, and if I were to be honest, that's a question I never answered. Not because I didn't want to or was too busy to bother, but because I would write an answer and then erase it. It just didn't feel like my response was right or that I even had one.

I got the jolt that prodded me to think about ethics when these issues impacted me at home. One of the absolute highlights of my day is to put my now-seven-year-old son to sleep. It's the time when he is the most honest with me and I am with him. From *who is the best clone trooper* to *why do girls in my class not like Star Wars*, we have had some intense discussions. One night, he confessed that while watching a kids' cartoon video on YouTube, he had seen an ad that had scared him and now he couldn't sleep. When I dived in, I could not explain how such an ad that used scary themes would be shown adjacent to kids' content. It was my industry that was responsible though. My son asked me a simple question: "Papa, can you tell YouTube people to not show ads that are scary?" I didn't respond but just hugged him, though my mind was doing a number on me: "Of course, love, but you see they give such low CPMs and I have committed those numbers on a procurement sheet somewhere."

These are a few examples of ethical questions many of us face or have faced and will continue to face. It's important to confront and acknowledge them because otherwise ethics becomes just a word that we put in our policy documents or PowerPoint slides, where we talk about data ethics and privacy as if by just saying it, we have all become ethical. It's also important because the generations that are getting into the workforce today have real concerns about some of these issues. And to them, they are existential questions. They should have been for our generation too. We were too busy chasing low CPMs, still are.

To brush up my knowledge of ethics before I could dive into advertising and data ethics, I read Professor Jonathan Haidt's *The Righteous Mind*. Haidt is the Thomas Cooley Professor of Ethical Leadership at the New York University Stern School of Business. The book itself has nothing to do with advertising or marketing at all; it seeks to explain why we are divided by politics and religion. I picked it up on a whim and I was grateful for it.

Professor Haidt dives into moral foundations theory, which to be honest I had never heard of prior to the book, but he had developed it with others such as Craig Joseph. When you're busy selling cigarettes, you don't pay attention to areas that you should.

The moral foundations theory posits that morality comes from moral intuition and not reasoning, as had been believed by many scholars in the past and had been the dominant belief in explaining how people made moral choices. In other words, your emotions matter when you make moral choices. Haidt identified six foundations:

- Care/Harm: What you instinctively experience when you see a cute cartoon or animal in distress
- Fairness/Cheating: The concept of justice, anger at being cheated on
- Loyalty/Betrayal: Why you back your sports team and get angry at people who betray you or your team or nation
- Authority/Subversion: Why you respect or fear your bosses or sometimes seek to undermine them
- Sanctity/Degradation: The concept of cleanliness, why certain ideas trigger disgust, like racism
- Loyalty/Oppression: Why you feel like banding together to resist tyrants and also why some others feel that they don't want too much government

Professor Haidt uses this theory to explain the choices that Republicans and Democrats make and why they make them. But it got me thinking about some of the ethical conundrums our industry faces and the choices we make. (By the way, read the book. It's one of the best I have read in a long time and takes complex concepts and presents them in an elegant, clean framework.)

One of the common themes I heard over and over from people I spoke to for this book was some version of this: We think that we are individually quite moral in our behavior, but our decisions are often at cross-purposes with what we truly believe in, and we seem to be stuck in a rut. In other words, as an industry, we tend to make choices that aren't good for either constituents of the industry or in the end for the consumers we claim to serve.

Of the six moral foundations, I found the first two helpful in explaining some of the issues we face today. Our Care/Harm foundations seem to operate at an individual or small cluster level or team level. As an industry, we don't seem to have an aspirational tone, a goal, or vision, like, for example, people working in medicine or self-driving vehicles or AI. I know I am generalizing, and while we are good at having a wonderful time in places like Cannes, folks in marketing who man the ships and operations would tend to agree with me. Our expressions of care extend to our team or friends or ourselves but fail to include in most cases the people we profess to care about: consumers. They are just insights and data points to be activated for a purpose.

As I got some downtime post my IPG stint, I started trying to be more social, attending more dinners and getting involved in some communities. I ran an experiment: in some cases, I would tell people that I worked in advertising, and in others that I was the data and tech guy who made advertising smarter. In the first case, I would be bombarded by questions around brands and which ads had I made. There was excitement and energy. In the second case, there would be some confusion around what I did and once I explained, there would be some form of concern around privacy and how I was able to get access to these datasets, and in other cases, there was outright despair around how their data was freely available. That's how consumers truly perceived my work. I cared about my team, my company, my strategies, goals, and the numbers (always the numbers), but not about the people on whom, to be quite truthful, I and my team depended on for growth.

The second foundation around Fairness/Cheating plays out in a very bizarre way in our industry. There is an underlying feeling of broken relationships and misaligned incentives all around. Go to Fishbowl, and you will read comments about how employees at agencies feel cheated by the long hours or how they felt that their work wasn't being appreciated fairly by clients. If you asked marketers, there is a lack of trust with certain vendors or tech platforms, and if you ask the vendors, they complain about payment terms. All of us believe that we are victims of unfairness, and it threatens to bedevil our industry and eat up the enthusiasm of people who look at the creative work and want to be a part of it.

I chanced upon a piece written by Tom Denford, CEO of ID Comms, in an industry trade magazine on the necessity for advertising ethics. As I had written before, we shared a common desire to look for differentiation and break the mold and hope that we could create better outcomes. I reached out to him, intrigued that the theory behind ethics and morality could find space in our industry.

He connected me to Andrew Sussman and the Institute of Advertising Ethics or the IAE. Andrew serves as its president and after an amazing chat, he invited me to get myself certified by the IAE in advertising ethics. To be absolutely honest, I thought this would be a breeze. I mean, I had spent twenty-five years in this industry, seen all kinds of shady situations, and even read up about the subject. Couldn't possibly fail.

I didn't. But I had to really think hard over certain concepts and questions. Because when you try to take these seemingly esoteric concepts and apply them in professional situations, you begin to understand the impact of your actions. In fact, I am hoping that Andrew isn't going to review my quiz scores. There were a couple of them where I was shocked to have made errors, and worse, when I retook the quiz, I still couldn't correct them!

There are nine principles of advertising ethics that the IAE has identified. Rather than mention the full text of each principle that you can find on their website,[34] I will just capture the gist here.

Be true and have high ethical standards when serving the public. (It sometimes needs reminding that our true clients are consumers.)

Exercise personal ethics when you are making or distributing commercial information to people.

Don't make people believe that ads are actually news or content or entertainment.

Be open about payments or free products given to social endorsers. Also, make sure everyone knows who your endorsers are.

Keep the nature of the audience and the product in mind. For example, are you talking to kids and are you trying to make them eat unhealthy stuff? There are principles from the food and beverage industry. Don't be a young Arun Kumar and waste time trying to skirt them. Try to make them stronger.

Don't compromise people's privacy but make it easy for people to change their data preferences. By now, you should know that much of this data doesn't truly help your brand, and there are workarounds coming up that will deliver even better outcomes than what has been produced so far.

Follow the laws and industry self-regulatory programs. Duh!

If you or your teams have ethical concerns, discuss them privately. Don't just quash the discussion. It's also a great way to attract new talent. This matters to them.

Be transparent with business partners; don't try to screw them with rebates and other incentives. But—and this is my addition, not that of the IAE—don't use payment terms to screw your partners.

---

34 https://www.iaethics.org/principles-and-practices.

None of this is rocket science, but when you think about its applications, you will find them challenging.

The question I get asked most about ethics and one that I have asked frequently as well is around whether all this even matters. We are a capitalist society; we have all signed up for it, and advertising and marketing are the spear's tip of driving consumption. Marketers and their ecosystem of partners are expected to drive growth and the fucking numbers and to do it within the boundaries of the law and that's that.

My aha moment was on a slide written by the IAE around the Ethics of Achievement. Ethics just isn't about feeling good on a personal level; it also signifies an achievement of attaining a higher standard, rising above the mediocre and producing solutions that work for more people. It's not just about what you put up on slides or what you tell your teams to make yourself feel better. Yes, it is about that. But it is primarily a mechanism of driving excellence. Being ethical is not a mushy, soft feeling that doesn't make any economic sense. The damn numbers are going to look better because if we actually get a bit more serious about using ethics as a guidepost while making decisions, people might actually like what we put out there. We could be wildly successful and do all this without having to hide what we truly do for a living during dinner parties.

Marketers and folks in agencies, tech platforms, and publishers have probably heard all this. But this message isn't just for them. It's primarily for CEOs and CFOs. If you are a CEO or CFO, just do one thing for me: the next time you see your kids (if you don't have kids, look for kids who are in the family or friends) stuck to their devices watching some short-form video that probably creates anguish for you because you're not sure it's appropriate and the medium is leveraging AI to groom your child's young mind to get addicted to content that is not healthy, reflect on your decisions. Were you the person who set cost-efficiency goals for your company's marketing team because that was an easy sell to the board or a metric that you could understand? Is yours one of the companies that, in search of the cheapest impression, finances the superior use of AI to drive hate speech and crap content to your own kids? If you are, call your CMO. Free her from this cost bullshit. Ask her to focus on what matters to your brand and to the people you claim to serve. Giving a little bit of thought will also help meet the damn numbers.

## Other Notable Efforts

There are other notable efforts, obviously, that many would consider pathbreaking work. I haven't highlighted many of them, especially the work that is being done inside the walled gardens. I'm sure they are awesome and really smart. But, unfortunately, it's very hard to peek under the hood and know what they have done. And even in cases where you do, the approach will work only on that platform. There is no connectivity with anyone else.

And I view efforts only through one lens: is it going to help the brand and the people it is looking to serve? When some of this work is viewed through that lens, it scores high but because the tactic and the underlying data do not travel, its applicability is limited to just one platform. And that, in my book, does not rise to the level I have used to judge the others. Except for the Meta example, which gives us a pointer to making AI work for us, I didn't feel inspired to mention others.

But there are a few honorable mentions that I would make.

Google's efforts over Topics definitely deserves a mention. The privacy sandbox initiative deserves support and the idea of utilizing a user's areas of interest based on browser behavior is workable. It remains to be seen, though, whether Google's efforts to assign random behaviors to a user to not let them get identified will impact accuracy of the audience. Google claims to do this to inject some randomness and make it hard to identify the user. There are parallels with the Meta effort.

Identity is another area where we might be able to get some better solutions than large central databases stitching together attributes basis hashed emails/zip codes or other identifiers. I spoke to Philip Shoemaker for my FairPlay podcast[35] around decentralized digital identity, the use of blockchain, and the ability of people to manage their own identity wallets. Philip worked on the Apple store with the late Steve Jobs and is now the CEO and founder of a nonprofit, Identity.com. I feel like there is much in this concept that could help, though a question that always arises with such concepts is whether people would make the effort to protect their identities.

I also love what Scope3 and Brian Kelly are doing to reduce carbon emissions from the media ecosystem. In fact, when I chatted with him for this book, he was quite categorical in surmising that a great approach would be to cut 50 percent of a brand's programmatic budget and taking a look at the impact on outcomes. The hypothesis is that a lot of the Open Web activity might not result in any impact loss but does create carbon.

I have deliberately skipped the retail media love affair that has begun. For the same reasons as skipping the walled gardens. There is no horizontality and I'm still not convinced that we have reached the point of avoiding incidental endogeneity in the data and spurious correlation. The area will mature and it will grow, but brands won't

---

35 https://forbesbooksaudio.com/episodes/phillip-shoemaker-the-man-behind-the-apple-app-store-and-identity-com-part-one/

get built-in retail media, and retail media cannot become the ultimate demand creation engine that a brand can be.

Hopefully, these two chapters have helped establish that there are a number of great initiatives, approaches, and practices that we already have, which can make data-driven marketing more valuable and effective. The next step is to codify them and create standards around some of these efforts. That is what I seek to do in the next chapter.

# CHAPTER EIGHT

# We Can Make It Better

A couple of years ago, I attended the American Advertising Federation's Annual Awards Gala. Everyone who was someone was there; many of us had purchased tables for our teams. And we were all well dressed to boot, as would be expected. As the awards were given out, there was a frisson of energy in the room as different people and teams were recognized for making outstanding contributions. And those contributions made us feel proud that we were part of this industry. For just a fleeting second, if we paid attention to the outcomes we could generate, then the world felt like a totally different place. It was the same feeling I got when I was a member of Cannes juries. Away from the obligatory rosés (I don't drink, so I haven't had one yet) to the fancy parties at the beach, you see evidence of thought and execution that are brilliant and reflective of some of the best minds in the business, many of whom were not at the beach with the rosés.

We create powerful and inspiring stories, and despite our best efforts to make it really hard and annoying for people to engage with them, we do create impact. It is in that spirit that I split this book into areas where we really fuck up and areas where we are either doing amazing work or have the potential to do amazing work. This chapter really is a distillation of all that you have read into a set of principles that we can follow to get better outcomes from our marketing budgets.

## The Approach

There are three interests, sometimes competing, that must be taken into account while designing principles by which we operate: that of people, that of the business or brand, and that of ethics. I'm deliberately keeping ethics as a third component. Because ethics, in my mind, represents the interests of society as a whole, an attempt to recognize that what might be good for people in the short term might not be great for us in the mid- to long term. (When you don't get plastic bags at your local supermarket, you are inconvenienced, maybe even intensely irritated. But plastic bags can clog the oceans, leading to a set of outcomes that negatively impacts all of humanity including you and your family.) I also recognize that ethics sometimes might set a standard that is impossible for a brand to meet, but it's better to aspire to meet a standard than disregard it totally. I'll take whatever we can get in this direction.

The purpose of these principles must be to strengthen a brand's relationship with its consumers; we are all collectively successful when brands are successful. There is no higher purpose for marketing to exist. Brands need to build relationships based on trust and within the parameters of the interests mentioned previously.

Lastly, I've made two fundamental assumptions: that platforms are not going to change their self-serving policies; neither is legislation going to catch up with them. Hence marketers must create their own world of trust and principles that do not depend on external sources to succeed. These principles need to include the following:

## 1. Less Is More

We have a tendency to collect as much information as we can about people. The belief is that there are signals buried there that we or AI can extract. And in some cases, there are; brands profit when they analyze granular data, but they also end up opening themselves to risk with respect to the data collected and abusing the privacy of people. And in many cases, there are no hypotheses that support the collection of that data. Brands need to move from a "more is better" to a "less is more" approach.

Have a hypothesis, and leverage data to prove or disprove the hypothesis. The challenge set for a CDO must be: What is the least amount of data needed to answer a brand's questions or challenges with a high degree of certainty? Every company can define its own standard of certainty, but I think a 70–80 percent range is fair. Adoption of this principle implies the following:

- PII can only be used for relationship management and for promoting new products to existing customers.
- Use contextual, interest, cohort, and content targeting for getting prospects.
- Data spines are only to be used for cleansing data. For example, if a brand has a database of customers but would wish to know more about them or fill gaps in the information, use data appends. Unless a brand has direct permission or expression of interest from consumers, do not use data spines to create audience profiles for prospects.
- Data deletion: Set data deletion standards and ignore the sixth sense telling you that you will need this six years from now.

You won't, just like you won't need the tax return from ten years ago.

- Restricted list: Create a list of attributes that your brand will not use for any purpose and declare that as part of the privacy policy. This has to be linked to the nature of the people the brand serves. The older they are, the more sensitive they will be to geo-location data for example. Calibrate to a brand's audience.

## 2. Technology Design

This might seem less relevant to marketers, but between analytics environments, cloud-based customer platforms, and AI, it's easy to lose perspective over implications of their build and their use. One of the references from Andrew Sussman was the Ethical OS.[36] The Ethical OS provides a framework of assessing future impact of today's tech and identifies eight risk zones that need mitigation. It's a great tool to figure out the impact of our tech stack and what we use even if we don't build it.

## 3. Ownership

Proactively allow people to access their data files to correct and own. Most regulations ask for this, but there is value in being on the front foot. It's quite possible that many people might choose to delete certain pieces of information but it's theirs after all. In any case, regulation is going to make it mandatory. It's best to get ahead of it.

## 4. Go Direct

Reduce the number of hops in activation and data transfer points. If you're using PII with permission for any contact, reduce inter-

---

36 https://ethicalos.org/wp-content/uploads/2018/08/Ethical-OS-Toolkit-2.pdf.

mediaries to one platform. There is a fair amount of work in this space around supply-side optimization and the like, but most of these efforts are focused on getting more value for the brand by having fewer intermediaries. The trick is in making sure that people get some value out of it too. If the brand saves on costs, don't spend on getting more useless impressions. Promotions and discounts are probably a better use for the budget, giving consumers some value in the end.

### 5. Horizontality Counts

Encourage initiatives or efforts to solve cross-platform or horizontal problems. There is no doubt that the ability of data science within the tech platforms is phenomenal, but it's outside where the expertise is needed the most.

### 6. Speak in Plain/Understandable Language

Take control over privacy policy information. Use plain English in describing data usage. NYT is a great example of using simple English to explain data usage. If you're using AI or generative AI, use English to explain how customer data is used.

### 7. Create clear connection points between aggregate models and granular information.

*If aggregate models are proved accurate, eschew granular data.* Work around models such as the movable middle must be encouraged. Map audiences to segments. Segment accuracy might be more relevant to a brand or a category at a point in time.

## 8. I could have just stopped with "Use AI," but there are multiple uses of AI that can drive a brand and its relationship to its audience.

- Use it to *limit collection of data*. Explore the creation of synthetic datasets that reduce the need to collect individual information that may not pertain to the use case. And *few-shot learning tactics* can help when datasets are not large. Volume alone does not determine the accuracy of a model; some of the best datasets within an organization relevant for marketing might come from panels or smaller research sets not sitting in central databases. They might be more valuable to train the AI on than other larger datasets. Paired with human insight, this is also a great approach in service of Principle 1: Less Is More.

- The one area where cost efficiency does play a role is in generating content and creativity. Use AI to *help create better creative stories* at a cost that allows for personalization. Creative quality drives brands and their profitability. As I cited the approach taken by Meta earlier, creative interactions can tell a lot about an audience.

- Use AI to *augment your marketing brain*. I couldn't think of a better description than "brain," but hear me out. Fragmentation of any sort is not going out of fashion anytime soon. Every walled garden will have AI-driven solutions but it will be driven for its own interests than for that of brands. On the other hand, with marketing budgets getting fragmented across departments and capabilities, complexity will only rise. AI has the potential to glean common behaviors, patterns, insights, and test hypothesis across pretty much all these available channels and activations and serve as the ideal partner for a CMO. No, it cannot replace a CMO. But it can augment a CMO's ability to make decisions faster and more intelligently. It will definitely impact the landscape of companies that work with a CMO but if used well, AI can clean up some of the mess that lies between brands and consumers. There is of course a greater probability of us allowing AI to drive a greater wedge between brands and their audiences but it's essentially up to us on how we bring AI to bear.

## 9. Drop Cost as a Way of Judging Effectiveness of Marketing.

It's like using the number of conversations between a married couple to assess the quality of a marriage or judging your child's education by the total number of classes she attended in a year. If, as a company, you're really serious about ESG, focus on the S for a bit. Does it make sense to pour all the money behind media and tactics that give you great cost-efficiencies but also fund dismantling a media-funding model that is essential for democracy? If people pay to avoid advertising or are prepared to not get news from outlets that use advertising to subsidize production cost, are we better off? If you're a CEO, take a good look around your leadership table and ask these questions. If you're an investor, pause and ask, What am I investing behind? Marketing dollars that are funding waste? Are you holding the management team to the right metrics? These seem obvious, so much so that I can see executives of most top companies dismiss these questions with a "been there done that" remark. But is that the case? I'm not convinced. And it doesn't seem like people are either. If you don't believe me, at your next dinner party….

The CMO council released a report on the state of marketing and finance collaboration.[37] The report said that when CFOs and CMOs collaborate, they are likely to focus on marketing analytics, machine learning, and automation over the next twelve months. Those who don't have the collaboration are focused on analytics, digital media, search, social media, brand marketing, and the like. When collaboration takes place, there is a future-facing approach; when there isn't, you're stuck in making today work better.

I like odd numbers; I am superstitious. Hopefully, while you were reading through these principles, none of them came across out of the blue. If you read through the previous two chapters, many of the points are just derivations. I've deliberately kept some technical approaches because I was conscious of making sure that readers could see the basis of the principle. I've tried to marry top-down and bottom-up approaches.

I'm sure there are better articulations of these principles, and maybe some of these principles should be challenged. I welcome the discussion and the challenges. But what I refuse to accept is that we have had these discussions and solved for them. Because we haven't. I also refuse to accept that these principles cannot be implemented because they are too technical or there are conflicting interests. Of course, there are. But that's what we need to battle, improve, and change. We cannot spend a trillion dollars and not have full control over it and make sure it is spent behind the right priorities.

---

37 Laurie Sullivan, "CMO Council Data Shows Concerns of Economy, CFO Collaborations," Mediapost.com, September 22, 2023, accessed October 19, 2023, https://www.mediapost.com/publications/article/389520/cmo-council-data-shows-concerns-of-economy-cfo-co.html.

# CHAPTER NINE

## And It All Comes to an End...

*Richard* sat in his study sipping his ice-cold Montauk. He was a beer guy when push came to shove; very few of his buddies knew that. He had a habit of keeping the truths about himself hidden in plain sight. His own motto centered around not having to reveal a truth unless you had no other choice.

He read the final pages of the Nielsen report again. After a grueling summer and many more heated discussions, he had managed to find some light. By bringing in a third party, he had removed some emotion and checkmated some of Sabiha's moves. His CFO had shown unusual aggressive tendencies in other areas of the business as well, and he had been searching for his own El Alamein to change the momentum. And marketing was just the right place to start. Too bad he had to lose Sarah over it. She had seen the introduction of the third party as a sign that she was not trusted by him and the team, which was not true. But she left despite Richard personally meeting with her and charting her future career path for her.

Nielsen had made three findings, at least according to Richard. He had a habit of boiling reports down to the three areas he must focus on or ignore. The superstition around the number three had existed ever since he had learned it was his deceased mother's favorite number. She had died when he was very young, and he used three to anchor himself to her.

The power of the airline's brand was crucial to maintaining sales, the Nielsen report had claimed: duh! Richard had been amazed that such a simple point had been a bone of contention, but his marketing and e-commerce teams had fought over this assertion. Turns out that it was true and the strength of the relationship was quite strong. Even though the airline was focused on a price-sensitive segment, people cared about the brand. But the messaging they had put out there was ineffective; it left people wanting more.

Audience choices were not that material to the final sale. This second finding was more shocking, but between the media agency, Stuart and Ross, and their teams, a fair amount of time and effort had gone behind fine-tuning audiences. Turns out that the variables they had identified didn't matter at all. In media activation, much of this had been diluted anyway. There wasn't even a consistent taxonomy of how these audiences had been defined. Some of the basic segmentation work they had done a year or two back probably needed to be dusted off and reintroduced to the teams. It had been an extensive piece of research that had been largely ignored in the audience creation process.

Lastly, there was a major issue of sharing data. While this was not a finding from the report, Richard had been keeping a close tab on its progress. Between Nielsen's constant complaints about data availability and Sarah's exit interview where she talked about how hard it was to get any data out of the commerce team, Stuart's stay at the airline was all but over. Not liking direct confrontation, Stuart had used any number of his underlings to create roadblocks and raise questions about the entire process. He probably thought that he had ears at the top and could get away from quiet sniping and undermining Richard's effort; it wasn't the first time that a senior executive had misjudged the power dynamics at the top.

But Richard could see that he had been part of the problem. By allowing the marketing function to get fragmented and budgets to get allocated between different departments, he had created a system of conflicting interests and zero-sum scenarios. He had allowed a greater voice for procurement and had agreed with their recommendations of focusing on getting the cost per acquisition down without understanding what was driving it up in the first place. While he was busy consolidating his position with the board, he had taken his eyes off the ball on marketing and sales, which come to think of it was as important as customer service, employee relations, and government lobbying. While the airline had grown by leaps and bounds over the last decade, some of its internal structures were still archaic, and he had fewer senior members in very senior positions that inevitably led to his own involvement.

He had to rejig and bring in some new talent. But first, he had to create one marketing team and make sure its capabilities were aligned with his expectations. And he had to figure out what to do with Stuart's team. Maybe bringing Ross's and Stuart's teams together would create redundancies, and he could push this through as a cost reduction measure? Whichever way he went, he needed a central analytics team that didn't feel pulled in two different directions. He wasn't convinced that Ross was the CMO he needed, but right now, he couldn't afford to let all his key execs leave.

As Richard shut the report, there was a nagging feeling that he had missed something. It was a deeply felt thought that he hadn't articulated for some time and had found its way into the report. He opened the report and shuffled through chapters until he found the comment that had struck a chord with him. Buried in page thirty-six of the seventy-five-page report had been findings from a set of focus groups conducted by Nielsen on consumer attitudes toward airline advertising. And one of the consumers had mentioned how she was fed up with being targeted by his airline's ads even though she would never fly business class and then being asked to buy a holiday package the next day as if the "airline was all over the place. They cannot make up their mind. What a waste!" He took out his black book; it was where he noted tasks that he absolutely had to do. His teams knew that if an item made it to the black book, it would have to get done.

*Speak to people who see my advertising*, he wrote.

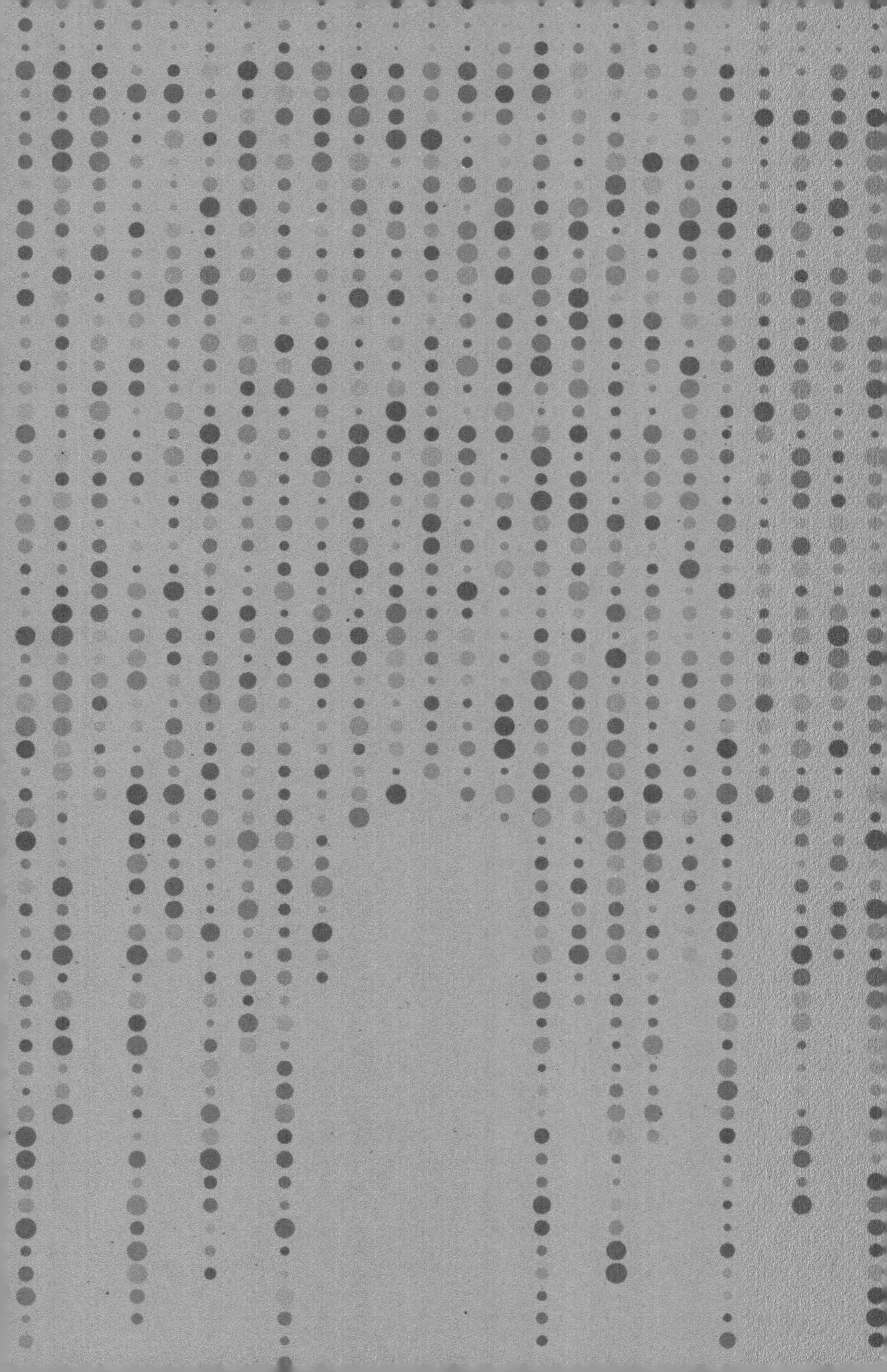

# EPILOGUE

A lot has happened since I began writing this book. Linda Yaccarino took over X, Krishan Bhatia has left NBC Universal, the Delete Act is making its way in California, more reports are out about TV measurement issues including Nielsen bringing in Amazon first-party data, the Google antitrust show is live in courts while the FTC has sued Amazon for monopolistic practices, Made-for-advertising websites have become a thing, and there are constant claims about AI-led innovation. With an election around the corner, one can only expect more headlines in the social space around disinformation, hate speech, censorship, bias, and the like.

I have deliberately chosen to not delve deep into the walled gardens and some of the innovations taking place in that space. They are worthy but, in my mind, are tarred with the brush of vertical excellence. Our industry needs to aspire to be better. We cannot rest on the abilities of a few to drive their own businesses while we wring our hands hoping for external intervention.

The last decade has been about getting the infrastructure in place to become more data driven and enabling some standardization to occur. Collecting data and making it available has, in some cases, trumped over the analytics itself, with the result that we either have waste in media or brands still come across like a punch-drunk dancer with two left feet to consumers who have proved to be savvier with both data and technology.

Don't take my word for it. Bob Liodice from the ANA did an analysis of the revenue and after-tax profits of Fortune 500 companies. He found that from 2000 to 2010, Fortune 500 companies had grown by 4 percent on average. From 2010 to 2020, that was 2.7 percent. During the greatest expansion of digital and data capabilities, the companies with the budgets to execute at scale and invest declined in growth.

It's safe to say that we haven't accomplished everything we set out to, but maybe we won't have to.

With AI rearing its head, maybe we don't need to connect the pipes horizontally. All we need is to train AI to understand the macro while staying connected to the micro. Imagine being able to forecast business impact while in market and keeping activation variables like cost pers under check. That's the opportunity; that is, if we don't first screw it all up by trying to make AI conform to our current world and current model.

That is the word of caution that marketers and their bosses should pay attention to. AI will not stop at making incremental change; it will disrupt completely, and it should be allowed to. If we do the hard work of creating the guardrails and setting the right objectives, we can have a hell of a ride and maybe even answer John Wanamaker's question correctly and consistently. Resistance to AI will be futile; it won't be as easy as removing specialists from organizations and pretending that the world will remain the same; you're either working with technology or you will be replaced by it.

Marketing, advertising, and brand building are crucial components of a capitalist society. And any society that believes in true freedom of speech will support a marketing ecosystem. And while the headlines and the polemics may not suggest so, people are still interested in advertising. It's a great piece of entertainment, a source of news and discussion, and sometimes exactly what you need as you seek to buy a product. There are concerns that the top 10 percent of the population in a market like the United States can buy themselves out of watching ads. If the ad-supported business model fails, it will lead to a reduction of both options and opinions in the market. Ironically, it is the much-maligned CMO and the marketing ecosystem that can either rise up to the occasion and demonstrate the power of the brand or not.

I have loved every minute of my twenty-five-year career and despite my many frustrations, there is no other industry I'd rather be in. But it is incumbent on us all to ensure that we don't allow the fact that we *can* overwhelm the question of whether we *should*.